THE SIXTIES

An American Family in Europe

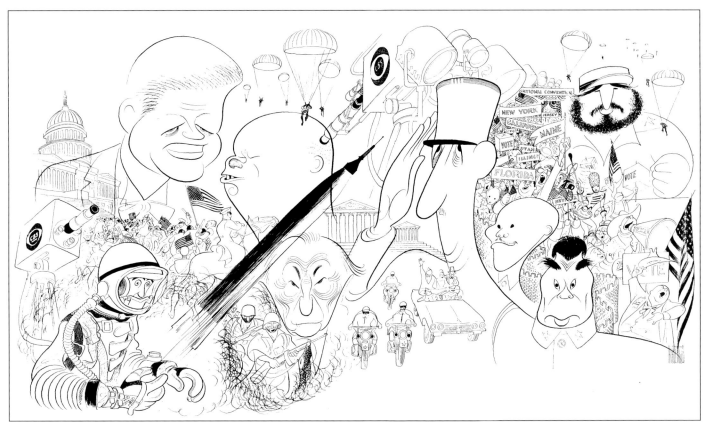

The Kennedy Years, 1962

World leaders intermingle with events of the early sixties, confirming the political tensions of the cold war, as portrayed in the superb line drawing by Al Hirschfeld. Included are (left to right) U.S. President John Kennedy; Soviet premier Nikita Khrushchev; Konrad Adenauer, "der Alte" (the old man), of West Germany; and French president Charles de Gaulle, here saluting in his general's uniform. Behind him are a bearded Fidel Castro of Cuba; a bald Chiang Kai-shek of Nationalist China; and bushy-browed Chou En-lai, the head of Communist China's People's Republic. Television is seen coming of age in its coverage of astronauts conquering space; mounted police quelling civil rights street protests; U.S. ground and airborne troops fighting in Vietnam; the president's motorcade; and the hoopla of a political convention, energizing the party faithful. With the Soviet withdrawal of nuclear missiles from Cuba in 1962, President Kennedy claimed that he wanted to be remembered as the man who kept the peace. His preferred epitaph would apply too soon. He was assassinated the following November. His successor, Lyndon Johnson, skillfully guided civil rights legislation but failed to end the Vietnam War.

The Sixties

An American Family in Europe

by

ADA FEYERICK

Academia Books

NEW JERSEY

2010

Academia Books, Inc.
15 East Hartshorn Drive
Short Hills, NJ 07078

www.adafeyerick.com

Book Design: Jerry Kelly
Picture Research: Jeanne-Françoise Roche, Paris
Copy Editor: Jaime Buerger

LIBRARY OF CONGRESS CONTROL NUMBER: 2009922497

ISBN 978-0-9653159-9-9

Printed in the United States of America

To my children and theirs after them.

AF

CONTENTS

CHRONOLOGY

Dates from the text

1905   France legislates separation of church and state.

1906   Alfred Dreyfus acquitted of treason.

1909   American Hospital inaugurated in Neuilly.

1919   Versailles Peace Conference.
        Ho Chi Minh appeals for Vietnamese independence.

1921   De Gaulle teaches history at Saint-Cyr military academy.

1936   Aviator Jean Mermoz disappears in airplane off African coast.
        Socialist premier Léon Blum legislates five summer vacation weeks.

1939   World War II: Germany invades Poland; Russia invades two weeks later.

1940   Paul Grüninger convicted in St. Gallen for falsifying entry papers of refugees.

1940-1944 France occupied by Germany.
        Vichy government headed by Marshal Philippe Pétain, Pierre Laval.

1940-41 Vichy's *Statut des Juifs,* exclusionary laws for Jews.

1942   Roundup of French Jews at the Velodrome d'Hiver.

1944   Antoine Saint-Exupery's plane disappears over occupied France.
        France liberated. De Gaulle's victory walk on Champs Elysées. Forms provisional government;
          visits Washington, D.C.

1945   Pétain sentenced to prison. Laval sentenced to death by firing squad.
        Ho Chi Minh appeals to President Truman for economic aid.
        France given Berlin control zone in defeated Germany by Allies.

1946   French colonial rule in Indochina.

1947-1983 Achille Peretti mayor of Neuilly.

1950   Soviet Union and China recognize Democratic Republic of Vietnam.

1951   Death of Marshal Pétain.

1954   French defeated at Dien Bien Phu. Geneva Peace Conference.

1956   Suez campaign to open Canal closed by Nasser of Egypt.

1957   United Nations Emergency Force (UNEF) established after French, English troops
        withdraw from Egyptian Sinai. Israel's Sinai campaign ends with UNEF in place.

        Treaty of Rome creates European Economic Community (EEC).

1958   De Gaulle elected French president.

The Sixties

1960   John F. Kennedy elected president.

1961   Failed U.S. Bay of Pigs invasion in Cuba; Berlin Wall erected.

1962   Russians withdraw missiles from Cuba.

        Algeria receives independence. *[We move to Zurich in December.]*

1963   Major Gordon Cooper orbits earth in Mercury capsule.

        President Kennedy in Berlin , *"Ich bin ein Berliner"* speech.

        Martin Luther King Jr. marches in Birmingham, Alabama, protesting bombing of
        Sixteenth Baptist Church.

        Civil rights march in Washington, D.C.

        [Steven born in Zurich.]

        Kennedy assassinated.

1964   France recognizes Communist China.

        Tonkin Gulf incident.

        U.S. troop increase in Vietnam War.

        Swiss Federal Council imposes labor and economic restrictions on foreign workers.

        American Week at Jelmoli in Zurich.

        China explodes atom bomb.

        Three civil rights volunteers killed in Mississippi.

        President Johnson elected; signs Civil Rights Act; appoints Warren Commission.

        Martin Luther King Jr. wins Nobel Peace Prize.

1965   *[Debby born in N.J. We move to France (Neuilly).]*

        Operation Rolling Thunder begins in Vietnam.

        Ho Chi Minh rejects U.S. peace offers during next two years.

        De Gaulle reelected for second seven-year term, opts for return to gold standard.

        Johnson signs Voting Rights Act.

        Watts riots, Los Angeles.

10

1966   De Gaulle gives NATO a year to leave France; visits Moscow.

French troops in Germany no longer under NATO command.

Periodic strikes in Paris.

Further U.S. troop increases in Vietnam War.

[Steven starts jardin d'enfants at Cours Montaigne.]

1967   NATO and SHAPE leave France for Belgium.

Hubert Humphrey visits Paris.

Egypt's President Nasser closes Strait of Tiran, demands U.N. forces leave Sinai.

Six-Day War in Middle East. France embargoes military weapons to Israel.

De Gaulle at Canadian Expo; *Vive Québec libre* speech in Montreal. Threatens boycott of Common Market.

H. Rap Brown heads Student Nonviolent Coordinating Committee (SNCC).

Four-day riot in Newark, N.J. *[We vacation in N.J.]*

Priests Philip and Daniel Berrigan deface draft records in Baltimore, Maryland.

1968   My Lai massacre of civilians by U.S. soldiers in Vietnam.

De Gaulle visits Romania and Afghanistan.

Johnson announces he will not run for president.

Days of May strikes in Paris by French students and workers. Sorbonne closed. De Gaulle flies to Baden-Baden to assure military support during strikes.

Martin Luther King Jr., Robert Kennedy assassinated.

Paris peace talks begin with U.S., South and North Vietnam.

Columbia University occupied by student radicals.

Gaullists win large majority in French elections.

France gains oil concessions in Saudi Arabia and Iraq. Iraqis to get Mirage jets.

Soviet troops invade Czechoslovakia.

Jean-Jacques Servan-Schreiber's *Le Défi Américain* published in English.

Richard Nixon elected president.

Pope Paul VI issues *Humanae Vitae.*

[Debby starts jardin d'enfants at Cours Montaigne.]

1969   Nixon orders bombing of Cambodia.

French union leaders call a general strike.

De Gaulle's referendum defeated. Retires to Colombey-les-Deux-Eglises.

Georges Pompidou elected president.

[Andrew born in Neuilly. We return to America.]

Apollo 11 and astronauts land on the moon.

11

After the Return

1970   De Gaulle dies suddenly on November 9th, a month after his book *Memoirs of Hope* is published.

1973   Vietnam cease-fire initialed in Paris. Death of Lyndon Johnson.

1976   Vietnam officially reunited.

Current Dates: from the Epilogue

1987   1st Palestinian intifada against Israel.

1989   Berlin wall falls.

1991   First Gulf War; Iraq fires Scud missiles at Israel. Soviet Union falls.

1995   Paul Grüninger, St. Gallen police chief, exonerated for aiding refugees.

1998   Swiss banks settle reparation claims.

2000   2nd Palestinian intifada against Israel.

2001   September 11 terrorist attack on U.S.
National Security Agency questions 1964 Tonkin Gulf incident.

2002   Bobby Frank Cherry convicted in 1963 Birmingham church bombing.
Switzerland joins United Nations.

2003   U.S. start of Iraq War March 19. Abu Ghraib prison scandal.

2005   Edgar Ray Killen convicted of 1964 manslaughter of three civil rights workers in Mississippi.
Haditha massacre of civilians in Iraq by U.S. soldiers.
France, Holland reject referendum to approve European Union constitution.

2006   Zacarias Moussaoui sentenced to life for his role in 9/11 attack.
President Bush signs 25-year extension of 1965 Voting Rights Act.
Hezbollah-Israel conflict in Lebanon.

2007   President Bush calls for more troops in Iraq (the "surge").
Nicolas Sarkozy elected president of France.

2008   Russian incursion into Georgia.
Barack Obama elected 44th U.S. President.

2009   Guantánamo to close. Special American envoy sent to Middle East.
Economic stimulus package passed.

PREFACE

The Sixties is a personal and political recollection of a decade that many believe was a turning point for America. During that period of watershed events, which still has bearing today, we had the unique opportunity of living abroad in Switzerland and France and learning to accept that different national interests often were at odds with those of our own country. How we settled in and coped as a family overseas is part of the story. How we reacted to those events, either witnessed first-hand or reported in the media, is the other. Letters written to my family in New Jersey add personal descriptions of the unfolding events. The Epilogue compares the sixties to the present, noting what has changed or remained the same in countries we once called home.

It was a time of great American economic expansion overseas, when tens of thousands of business and professional men and women worked in subsidiary companies, the majority with families in tow. By favorable chance, we were to live first in Zurich and then Paris, or rather, the nearest Paris suburb of Neuilly. In 1963, ten months into our two-year stay in Zurich, the birth of a son became our happiest memory, President John Kennedy's assassination the saddest. With a second baby, this time a girl, we moved to Paris for the next four years, in the heart of local and world politics dominated by French president Charles de Gaulle, pursuing his independent, political path up to 1969, when he retired from public life after a failed referendum.

The book combines memory and research. To the historian Carl Becker, memory is a guide to the present and a path to the future. Without memory, he claimed, there is no knowledge, and that which was not personally experienced should be supplemented with original research. Memory here includes both a close-up view of President de Gaulle in his chosen role as arbiter between the two superpowers, the United States and the Soviet Union, and also a distant view of America's domestic turmoil and foreign involvement in Vietnam. Unrest on college campuses, mainly due to the military draft; cities in flames due to frustratingly slow civil rights progress; and the assassinations of President John Kennedy, his brother Robert, and the Reverend Dr. Martin Luther King Jr., reflected the country's deep malaise. The historical research urged by Carl Becker includes America's lost opportunities for avoiding the Vietnam War; de Gaulle's mistrust of his allies during World War II, as well as neutral Switzerland's official policy toward refugees from Nazi-occupied countries; and the origin of France's policy of secularism. Although the minority populations of Jews and Huguenots were emancipated after the French Revolution, for the sake of unity, loyalty to the Republic took precedence over religious beliefs and ethnicity.

Europe was war-weary. The age of colonialism was ending. Western Europe was redirecting its energies toward a united, economic effort, finally facing the futility of its historic wars and the waste of its youth in battle. In Switzerland, we wondered if its protected status as banker to the world would enable it to remain uninvolved in world affairs indefinitely. In France, we wondered if the influx of Muslims from North Africa after Algerian independence in 1962 would have an impact on her secular policy and whether her antiquated educational facilities were adequate for a new generation. We had to cope with de Gaulle's anti-Americanism, although he declared that if America ever was threatened, France would be its ally.

De Gaulle's concern was an America that he believed was as much of a threat to peace, with its military might and self-image as democracy's champion in Southeast Asia, Africa, and the Middle East, as its Soviet cold war foe. He called the Vietnam War unjust and detestable, "leading a great nation to lay waste a small one." The United States was described by the writer Sanche de Gramont as a giant stumbling around with a bag over its head, with President de Gaulle as the self-appointed giant killer. Some called their disagreements a family feud, but as France's criticism escalated, the "family" seemed dysfunctional. André Malraux, the minister of culture in de Gaulle's cabinet, described America as the most powerful country on earth without wanting to be, which is why it "makes war well and peace poorly."

And what of the French, convinced of their cultural superiority? We had the opportunity of observing the formation of their character, beginning with the country's earliest teaching methods, as our children began their schooling in the Cours Montaigne in Neuilly. An unbending conformity in the classroom carried over to the workplace, where a strict hierarchy was often the source of labor's frustration. Frequent strikes for better working conditions and pay occasionally left us without electricity or public transportation. The Days of May in 1968, when striking unions sympathized with students from the Sorbonne, rioting on the Left Bank for academic improvement, was a French wake-up call for modernization. Our reaction to the strikes was shared by de Gaulle who, in impatient moments, found the French to be ungovernable and ungrateful.

In the United States, President Lyndon Johnson was the tragic figure caught in the web of the Vietnam War at the expense of his Great Society social programs and civil rights legislation, for which he most wanted to be remembered. His decision not to run for president in 1968 confirmed his profound disappointment in how his hopes for his presidency had failed. His successor, Richard Nixon, wrote in his memoirs that Johnson was president at the wrong time. He might have been a great peacetime president, but the war abroad and at home proved too much for him.

14

Rather than using familiar photographs that appeared in the media during the sixties, political cartoons from various countries were chosen to give a different, local view of events:

From America, Pulitzer Prize-winning cartoonist Herblock (Herbert Block) offers a perspective on the results of slow civil rights progress in the major cities. To him, the political cartoon was a reminder that elected officials have a responsibility to the public they serve. Bill Mauldlin, another Pulitzer Prize winner, focuses both on American shortcomings and on what he knew best – soldiers at war. His philosophy of cartooning was "circle and stab, circle and stab."

From England, Vicky (Victor Weisz) captures the burden of the presidency as it was thrust on Lyndon Johnson.

The superb French cartoons, or *dessins,* mainly from *Le Canard Enchâiné,* the weekly satirical newspaper, highlight the nation's foibles in politics and society, as do those in *Paris Match* and the now defunct *Combat.* The cartoonists, in what might be considered France's golden age of cartooning, include Moisan (Roland Moisan), LAP (Jacques Laplaine), Effel (François Lejeune), André Escaro, and Morez.

The Middle East journal *Al-Hayat* gives an ironic view of the impending conflict with Israel months before the outbreak of the Six Day War in 1967.

A month after our return to America in the summer of 1969, our astronauts walked on the moon. New worlds were opening. After a six-year absence, our new world was our own country awaiting rediscovery.

One simple truth remains. The uninhibited, open-hearted outreach of children to new friends of different languages and nationalities in foreign lands is the key to the door of the world.

[I]
ZURICH

With snow-covered Alps above the lake, the Zurichsee, and the tranquil Limmat River flowing between both banks of the town, Zurich was in sharp contrast to the concrete and glass skyscrapers of Manhattan. The independent Swiss enjoyed their quality of life and took pride in their long history from prehistoric to modern times, as shown by the artifacts and art in the National Museum on the west bank (right foreground). Its neo-Gothic tower rises over the railway station at the northern end of the Bahnhofstrasse, the main street, where Swiss banks form the economic center of the country. On the east bank of the Limmat (left) toward the lake, it was in the double-towered Grossmünster cathedral that Huldrych Zwingli preached the Reformation.

In January 1963, the Lake of Zurich froze, the first time since 1929. Special train service brought thousands of ice skaters into Zurich, and on any given Sunday while the freeze lasted, there were a hundred and fifty thousand people crowding the twenty-five miles of the lake's surface. *The Weekly Tribune,* the only English language newspaper in the city, called it "Europe's Largest Skating Rink," frozen from end to end.

As we walked back and forth across the lake, marveling at the phenomenon, I wondered how I could bear this freezing cold country another day, even though I had only been there a month. The frigid European winter, the coldest in a century, curtailed power production due to the low levels of water in the rivers. In Zurich, we were urged to ration electricity each night after 8:30 P.M.

Philippe and I had been married a few weeks before in New York. I remembered sunny Puerto Rico where we had gone after the wedding and wished that I could have taken even one of its rays with me to brighten Zurich's gloom. Seven hours after leaving Idlewild airport in New York, our Swissair plane was diverted to Geneva instead of landing at Zurich's Kloten airport. Zurich's location between low mountains afflicts it with winter snow, ice, fog, and whatever other poor landing conditions are considered sufficient to reroute a plane to a more favorably endowed Swiss city. We took a five-and-a-half hour train ride to Zurich that night. After a total of fifteen hours of travel, we made a weary entrance after midnight into our apartment on the Forchstrasse.

Philippe, Belgian born, now an American citizen, had been working in Zurich for a year at the Swiss office of White Weld, a Wall Street investment bank on Claridenstrasse. Together, we were 2 out of 643 Americans living and working in the city during the sixties, mainly in American affiliates, or, as the organized Swiss broke the numbers down, 367 men and 276 wives.

Some of the large American firms in Switzerland, such as Chrysler, Alcoa, Du Pont, and the research facilities of RCA, Union Carbide, and IBM, were there for its central location in Europe, good transportation, banking, and academic facilities. Zurich certainly met those criteria. But there were rules to remember, such as those that were printed as a courtesy for American businessmen by Pan American World Airways: Never see a European without an appointment, especially the Swiss and Scandinavians who wait for a client "with a stop watch." Southern Europe was a little more lenient. And don't talk business at lunchtime. Europeans like to enjoy their meals.

Zurich. It was the one major city I skipped during my *wanderjahr,* a year of traveling abroad after college. There is nothing here of interest, I was told, a city of banks and bankers attracting depositors from all over the world. It was not uncommon to see saffron-robed, sandal-clad Buddhist monks from Southeast Asia strolling down the Bahnhofstrasse. "Checking up on their money," as a friend remarked. As banker to the world, Switzerland was assured of its neutrality.

The "gnomes of Zurich" is a term that seems to have originated in 1964 with the Labour prime minister of Great Britain, Harold Wilson, who blamed the weakness of the pound sterling on the manipulations of a few leading Swiss bankers. The phrase came to refer generally to a powerful group of bankers and financiers in Zurich who were engaged in foreign exchange speculation. Swiss secret numbered-accounts were believed to be the domain of savvy business tycoons, deposed or current political leaders, or drug dealers. My paltry savings and American Heritage stock from my working days in New York did not qualify in the numbered-account category.

My first newlywed task was to rearrange the lovely apartment in a concrete, modern building that Philippe had found near the Enzenbuhl Friedhof, the next-to-last tram stop on the Forchstrasse overlooking the Zurich lake. The blue Number 11 tram became our lifeline to the lively city center. The cocktail glasses on the first shelf, used for a bachelor's after-work drink invitations, were now moved to the third shelf and replaced by dishes for the dinners yet to be.

The other task was to become comfortable in a foreign country and a new language. My only knowledge of German was an intense, three-month night school course at New York University before leaving for Zurich. I had already learned "Where is the railroad station, please," and "I would like to buy an apple." I could now travel by train and buy fruit.

20

In the current twenty-six cantons of Switzerland, joined in loose confederation, the four official languages are German, French, Italian, and Romansch, even though this last language is spoken only by 1 percent of the population in the canton of Graubünden. Of the four choices, in Zurich I would have to grapple, not with pure German, but the Swiss-German dialect of *Schweizerdeutsch.* It would take true grit to learn.

Shopping was a challenge. There were a few embarrassing moments, such as asking the salesgirl at Séquin Dormann, an upscale home-furnishing store on the Bahnhofstrasse, *"Was ist Liebe?"* The directions said to wash my newly purchased stainless steel pot *"mit Liebe."* Was it Brillo, Ivory soap, Ajax? She blushed, then blurted out, *"Amour."* Mit Liebe meant washing the pot with love and gentle care. I hastened home to wash my pot lovingly. It was in Jelmoli's *Lebensmittel,* the amazing supermarket on the *sous-sol,* or basement, of this central department store with products from all over the world, that I asked a store clerk which oranges were best for mustard, having confused *senft* (mustard),with *saft* (juice). The next day, I phoned an American girl who gave German lessons.

Of the 276 American wives on record in Zurich, I met none. Our social life was mainly office-generated. The American Women's Club was not as organized as it is today but did manage to put out a small, useful booklet about shopping, commercial establishments, doctors, and becoming acquainted with Zurich. They were only suggestions, not endorsements. Social events were not included.

The population statistic for baby output in Switzerland in 1963 was about nineteen per thousand. It was to become one more when I learned that in October we were to have a baby. How to find an obstetrician in Zurich? I was fortunate to have the name of the founder of the natural-childbirth method in Switzerland, Dr. Thomas Rust. He spoke perfect English, a bonus for this non-German-speaking American who had to follow sensible medical instructions for nine months.

Natural childbirth classes suggested by Dr. Rust became a weekly routine. He told me that it was better to know what to expect, "like knowing what is necessary to climb an Alp." It was March, and although the baby was not due until October, I trudged to class each Tuesday and waited for the female instructor to teach us how to relax, count, breathe, and hold it for the big push. I must have been her star pupil. In the relaxing phase, with her soothing voice telling us *langsam, langsam,* slowly, slowly, I would fall fast asleep. One of the other pregnant women nearest to me would gently nudge me awake so I could pay attention and climb that Alp.

For a mental stretch, there were courses at the Jung Institute. Carl Jung, the famous psychiatrist and once a resident of neighboring Kusnacht, had an unfriendly parting of the ways from the original teachings of Sigmund Freud and started his own school and new approach to the study of the unconscious. The words animus and anima, the male and female inner force within the opposite sex, were new words to learn. The professors at the school were Jung's female disciples. My instructor brought her enormous, lethargic dog to school to sleep under her desk while she taught. I wondered how much that hound knew. Other Americans were studying at the Institute to become Jungian analysts. In America, their center was on the West Coast, unlike the Freudians who monopolized the East Coast. It seemed an intelligent way of sharing the analytic wealth.

We kept up with the news in the *International Herald Tribune (The Paris Trib), The New York Times,* and various American magazines, such as *Time, Newsweek,* and *U.S. News & World Report,* as did most Americans abroad. A visiting cousin noted with amusement that if someone started a sentence about a news item in *Time,* someone else in the room could finish it.

Guten abend, Liebe Zuschauer, "Good evening, dear viewer," began the evening news on German television, our local source of information. We strained nightly to hear what was happening in America. Even from its neutral position, the Swiss were uneasy about talks between America and the Soviet Union regarding a nuclear test-ban treaty. Switzerland had refused to sign it. Only Japan, India, the Arab Republic, and Israel went along with the nuclear Big Three – the U.S., Great Britain, and the Soviet Union. French president Charles de Gaulle's veto of Great Britain's entry into the Common Market added to Swiss misgivings. They did not know where Europe was heading. Would it become isolationist? Would the friction between de Gaulle and the U.S. impact badly on Europe? Would America reduce its combat troops in Germany, thus encouraging a Soviet confrontation? What the Swiss did care about was controlling inflation; worldwide tariff cuts, which would favor European exports; owning one's own home; and keeping the dollar strong. The rate of exchange at that time was 4.35 Swiss francs to the dollar, favorable to us living in Switzerland and to American tourists enjoying the scenery.

The year 1962 was a calm period in America's history, described as "more peaceful than at any time in nearly thirty years" – the calm before the storm. When we arrived that year in Europe, there were still memories of the failed anti-Castro invasion attempt by Cubans in Miami to the island's Bay of Pigs in April 1961. America was accused of not providing effective air cover for the invaders, who subsequently ran out of ammunition, a blot on John Kennedy's Camelot. In an American face-off with Premier Nikita Khrushchev, the Soviets blinked. A year later in October 1962, they withdrew their missiles from Cuba, their client state. Some analysts felt that World War III had been prevented.

The cold war was on. Soviet Russia was the enemy, often described in the American press as a country that fished in troubled waters, be it in Cuba, or in areas important to

American strategic interests. Political confrontations with the U.S. were commonplace, although military action was mutually not an option.

In the sixties, America had sharp disagreements with its Allies, especially on Europe's defense and nuclear strategy. President Kennedy said he couldn't worry about hurt feelings. The U.S. was paying most of the bills, and he would pursue his policies whether the Allies liked them or not. Swiss foreign-affairs specialists agreed, declaring that Americans should not expect to be loved by the whole world. "Americans tend to take setbacks abroad too seriously and talk themselves into a crisis of confidence." They felt we should take even a firmer stand on Cuba and Berlin, and with Moscow on the nuclear test-ban agreement.

President de Gaulle wanted to keep Europe free of American influence. Within the next few years, he positioned himself between America and the Soviet Union, seeking European leadership, the underlying incentive to his foreign-policy decisions. He dealt directly with Soviet Russia's satellite states; championed his own nuclear force, the *force de frappe*, rather than combining efforts within the established framework of NATO (North Atlantic Treaty Organization); and did not pay his share of United Nations bonds to cover France's costs in the Congo. De Gaulle's decisions perturbed Washington. As of 1965, we were to live through many of these events firsthand in Paris.

Yet there were gratifying times for Americans in Europe. One of President Kennedy's future goals was to have a man on the moon in five years. On May 1, 1963, Major Gordon Cooper made twenty-two orbits in his Mercury capsule. The door to the conquest of space was opening.

On June 20, President Kennedy made a trip to Europe. One of his important stops six days later was a visit to Chancellor Konrad Adenauer of West Germany and his designated successor, Ludwig Erhard. Kennedy assured them of America's protection. As he stood before a crowd of 1.5 million in West Berlin, he caught the public mood in his famous phrase, *Ich bin ein Berliner* – "I am a Berliner" – spoken with his familiar Boston accent. To the Germans who claimed that they could work with the Communists, Kennedy stated, "Let them come to Berlin." His meaning was clear. Free people lived and worked in democratic West Berlin. East Berlin was still under the Soviet thumb. Let the Russians come and see what democracy had accomplished in the West. America was the defender of Europe against communism with its five divisions facing east.

My letter home after Kennedy made his Berlin speech confirmed, "It was a proud time to be an American in Europe." Six months later, on a Christmas day President Kennedy would never see, two East Germans were shot trying to escape over the wall that separated East from West. It raised the total to sixty-eight who had been killed at the wall since it was built in August 1961.

The cynical Swiss reaction to President Kennedy's trip was that with the almost $4 million in U.S. aid that Germany received between 1945 and 1962, the Bonn government would continue to pay "lip service to America while quietly cooperating with France." The Swiss advice was to discuss and settle all disputes with Charles de Gaulle in order to make the Atlantic partnership work.

Yet there were clouds on the American horizon. The civil rights movement was gathering momentum. The Negroes, soon to be called Blacks or African-Americans by their own preference, were becoming impatient with the slow pace of legislation on their behalf. From 1956 to 1963, there had been sixteen bombings of Negro homes and churches in Birmingham, Alabama. The Reverend Doctor Martin Luther King Jr. rallied the Negro community in mass protests and picketing demonstrations, determined to desegregate facilities in downtown department and variety stores and to see that a biracial committee was appointed to work together for the common good. Hundreds were arrested, including Dr. King, with the police using brutal means to stop their progress. In mid-May, I wrote home with reactions to the televised events:

> The situation in Birmingham had me crying the other day. German television showed dogs attacking the Negroes and one woman being swept off her feet by a high-powered water hose. Is it really happening? Today, the *New York Times* reported the bombings. Is it true that Kennedy can't step in since it's not a breach of federal law? So he says, but surely he can find a loophole and stop the white hoodlums before the Negroes decide they have had it and get drastic. But I think they will win slowly but surely. Can't we give Alabama back to the Indians?

The civil rights march of two hundred thousand supporters, both black and white, in Washington D.C. on August 28, 1963, clearly showed that the Blacks had found their voice. On September 15, in a White backlash, Birmingham's Sixteenth Baptist Church was bombed. Four young black girls died. Their deaths deeply affected President Kennedy. Civil rights legislation took form.

Then there was Vietnam in Southeast Asia. American soldiers asked, "What were we doing here, anyway?" The "falling domino theory," as President Eisenhower and his secretary of state, John Foster Dulles, called it in the fifties, related to those weaker Southeast Asian countries that could fall to the Communists if there was no containment. This did not seem to be a sufficient reason for what GIs saw as a bottomless pit in this twenty-year-old civil war between North and South Vietnam. The Communist Vietcong, guerrilla forces in South Vietnam, opposed American efforts to shore up the South Vietnamese government of Ngo Dinh Diem.

Our forces called it "McNamara's war" after Robert McNamara, the eager secretary of defense both under Presidents Kennedy and Johnson. The war was variously described as dark, vicious, and bogged down in the swamps of Vietnam. Our servicemen perceived the regime of South Vietnam's Diem as corrupt, intolerant of his country's Buddhists, and our backing of him as ill-advised. Ho Chi Minh, leader of North Vietnam, stated that since the French were defeated in six years, and since America was twice as strong, it might even take twelve years. But he added, "With America's lack of staying power for the kind of war Communists wage, it may take less time than that."

Although close friends were scarce, we had met one compatible couple. He was an expatriate American writer, Eugene Epstein, who made Switzerland his occupation. He had originally come to Basel as a music student, worked in New York as a writer-producer for WQXR, and eventually settled abroad permanently. His book jackets described him as Switzerland's resident humorist. His wife, the beautiful Maud, originally from Germany, was a gifted linguist, pianist, and gourmet cook. They had a cozy house filled with books and music in Feldmeilen, a few miles south of Zurich, with a view of the lake. Gene referred to his two children, Michael, a lawyer, and Deborah, a theater actress and producer, as his "dynasty."

Gene and I became friends. I was the new American temporarily in Switzerland. He was the increasingly restless expatriate who wondered if he would ever go home again. We discussed publishing, which we both knew well. His love of Chinese food was legend. From his writings I could detect a growing homesickness. In his fourth book, *Malice in Wonderland,* Gene was to write, "It seems inane that we should have left the United States, a country of some two hundred million, for the prime purpose of meeting a handful of our countrymen in Switzerland. But that's the way it was." As for the Swiss, Gene called them humorless. In *Take Me to Your Chalet,* he quoted a fictional Swiss who asked, "Don't you understand a Swiss joke when you hear one?" Answer (probably reflecting Gene): "I'm not sure I ever heard one." In his last book, *A Pain in the Alps,* Gene concocted an imaginary conversation reflecting a Swiss attitude toward anyone not Swiss.

What gives you foreigners the right to criticize us when you know that we are better than you? You also know that we do everything right – but absolutely everything! So why are your American country people not impressed – or do they think it even matters what they think? I will never understand why people don't love us just because we are so perfectly perfect! . . . Yes, we can accept a word of constructive criticism, but not that garbage about our being stingy, rigid and reserved! Why shouldn't we be skeptical toward foreigners? Can they really be trusted? The way you can trust a Swiss? Well?!

One incident proved Gene's point. I had taken my woolen coat to a dry cleaner listed in the American Women's Club booklet. It was heavy and warm, especially bought with Zurich winters in mind. It came back from the cleaner with a shredded lining. Where was I supposed to find a coat that fit me in my pregnant condition and on such short notice? The owner of the establishment firmly told me that if I had any complaints I could take them to the head of the dry-cleaning factory in St. Gallen, and he would abide by his decision. The fault, he said, was in the material.

Philippe and I made an appointment one Saturday to go the distance to St. Gallen. Surely the factory manager would see that the coat was in perfect condition and sympathize with this expectant mother. The manager tested the fabric, and after two hours we were summoned. The verdict: inferior material, incapable of standing up to Zurich's impeccable dry cleaning.

Craftsmanship Around the World

The American reputation for inferior workmanship is inferred in the above cartoon, in which Swiss, Swedish, and Japanese products tower above a car produced in the U.S. by indifferent workers, run by undisciplined unions, that could paralyze industry with their labor demands. The Swiss not only took pride in the quality of their goods, but unions in Switzerland rarely, if ever, stopped work nationwide.

As social unrest grew in America, Switzerland was having its own economic problems. Its major fear, inflation, was due to a rise in wages of 15 percent and living costs of 8 percent. The purchasing power of the Swiss franc was half of what it was twenty-three years earlier when World War II started. For us, however, the rate of exchange of 4.35 Swiss francs to the dollar was a boon to our ability to meet our living expenses and for the baby to come. In this country of 5.4 million people, there was no unemployment. About five hundred thousand workers, mainly from Italy and Spain, had to be imported to work on the construction of high dams in the Swiss Alps. The Swiss found that the Spanish were good workers. The Italians were another matter, accused as they were of polluting the water in Zermatt.

The foreign influx required new housing, schools, transportation, and public services for their families. Shortages pushed up prices. Swiss factories could not keep up with consumer demands, and imports were needed to make up for the scarcity. It was only the flow of foreign capital into Switzerland that kept the country from a large balance of payment deficit.

To protect against the problems of inflation, a shortage of office workers, a housing scarcity, and rising costs in service industries, the Swiss Federal Council began to put a lid on work permits for foreigners who could hold the more skilled jobs in the country. They would be granted only where the total staff of a firm would not increase more than 2 percent. Residence permits for American employees in the four hundred to five hundred subsidiary firms in the major cities would also be limited. Philippe had an easier time getting a labor permit than a co-worker who came a year later. A one-year moratorium was declared on unnecessary buildings, such as museums, theaters, or nightclubs, and private homes worth more than $50 thousand. Even funds for public housing were curtailed. "A cannon to shoot down a sparrow," claimed *Newsweek Magazine*, but the people were expected to, and did, support the measures.

Inflation or not, as my October baby due date approached, there was comfort in living in this neutral, stunningly beautiful country. Dr. Rust had advised that calm walks in the woods were necessary to bring fresh air to my unborn child. "The baby," he said, "is organizing itself." The stately fir trees and the pure air above the lake of Zurich were far from the canyons of New York. I loved them both, but new chapters were unfolding. This was the best place to be, a point driven home when I received a letter from a former colleague in New York complaining about the pressures of publishing deadlines. She wrote, "New York is keeping me far busier and more neurotic than I care to be. It used to be that I had to work for two, now I find I'm working for three. I would readily switch roles with you. Let me know if you need a babysitter."

I decided to take my driving test in order to be more mobile in case of emergency after the baby was born. Fitting myself behind the wheel in my eighth month was a challenge, as was the dour face of my driving instructor. He almost seemed ready to fail me if I did not show enough respect for the twenty-five page Swiss road manual, which was distributed on my first enrollment day. The written test would include mathematical formulas of speeds necessary to pass another car, and true-false and essay questions. Finally, there was the practical road test, driving up a preselected steep hill outside of the city center and parallel parking with the front wheel turned toward the curb to make sure the car did not roll down.

The day for the test came. I had the mathematical formula down pat. It was the steep hill that worried me. My dour instructor was nervous as I drove up the hill and watched for oncoming cars, checking the side and rearview mirrors as the manual required. The directional signal was on, I pulled to the curb, set my wheels against it, and waited. I passed. Only then did the nervous instructor loosen up, as relieved as I was. "Did you enjoy the test? Do you think it is a fair test?" I assured him that the test was just *wunderbar.* I got my license, then drove into town to break the news to Philippe. He promised that if all went well, or even if it did not, we would go to see *Lawrence of Arabia* in the cinema near his office. I was giddy with success. Peter O'Toole was dashing on his tan camel and the desert was serene, but nothing compared to our blue Peugeot and the fir trees of Zurich. I had passed the notoriously tough Swiss driving test.

As the Swiss are diligently well prepared, I was told to go to a course for pregnant mothers in which bathing, dressing, and feeding a baby was demonstrated on a doll. Newborn infants here were wrapped in five heavy pieces of flannel. I told the teacher I had never seen anything like it. She said, "American babies have too little on, and the crib is always wet." The teacher then informed us that 50 percent of Italian babies die from infection of the navel before it heals. That evening I wrote home complaining about my instructor: "I think she's insane. You don't have to dress a baby like that, especially with rubber mattress covers." And regarding the infant mortality of Italian babies, "I was quite upset." Cultural differences were apparent.

On the morning of October 17th, I knew that things were underway. Philippe had just come back from a business trip to Scandinavia, fortunately just in time. We went to Dr. Rust's office only to be told by the nurse that he was out of town. But I was assured that the doctor on call was capable. Totally strange doctor, foreign country, contractions – not a situation devoutly to be wished.

I was in the Hirslanden Klinik at 2 P.M., where, we had been told, Arab sheiks send their wives to give birth. Midwives were the norm in Switzerland, as was *lachtgaz,* a mask that was put over the expectant mother's face during natural childbirth when the pain got too intense. Since the word meant "laughing gas," I expected to have a laughing fit at any moment. Not only was this not funny, but the midwife would run over with her hearing instrument, the kind deaf people used to hold to their ear yelling, "What did you say?" pressing it hard on my stomach to listen to the baby's heartbeat each time there was a strong contraction. While she did her best to help in German, she did manage to keep repeating one word in English at the proper time, "Push."

At 7:15 P.M., Steven Jeremy was born. He was presented to me wearing white cotton mittens, a precaution in case his fingernails scratched his face. The nurses had placed a pink bonnet on his head. In Switzerland, pink was for boys. The care was superb. The length of stay was a full week, (unlike the current American two-day hospital rush). A Swiss bonus was a daily visit from a personal trainer to get the stomach muscles back in shape. She was the Valkyrie Brünnhilde without the spear or armor, a tall, blonde, strapping, exercise guru. She threw open the window on chilly mornings and set about instructing me in stomach crunches. I would have preferred to spend the time worrying about how I would cope once I got home, even refusing the nurse's suggestion to dress and walk in the garden where the leaves were turning autumn colors on those beautiful October days. Except for Philippe, there was no family to stop by or offer me well-meaning advice. I was on my own. The new dad's first official duty was to go to the American consulate to register his son's birth and apply for his passport.

Schwester (Sister) Katya, whom we had hired for two weeks when I returned home, was a superb, highly trained, Swiss baby nurse. She managed to get Steven off the 2 A.M. feeding, much to my relief. I did not ask how she did it, but it was nice to sleep through the night. I think the secret was a few ounces of sugar water to tide him over until the next bottle at 6 A.M.

Before leaving, she gave me written instructions for Steven's daily schedule. "You must follow these to the letter and not go by what the doctor says, or else I won't give them to you," she warned. I promised, and off she went. But I had my Dr. Spock baby book on hand for ready reference.

Nine months later, another defining moment took place. Philippe and I were invited to Belgium to visit his family, leaving Steven in the care of Katya for a few days. He was on a three-meal-a-day schedule now, making life easier. When we returned, much to my horror, Katya had put him back on her original four-meal plan. At lunch on her last day, she forced a spoonful of fruit into his mouth, for which she was promptly rewarded with its return. She was mortified. I felt validated. Katya was capable, but her undeviating schedule did not suit Steven's tranquil nature. It took ten days for him to settle down to his usual happy self. We were not going anywhere for a while.

After she left, I received a letter. Gene, the Swiss observer, could have predicted it. She preferred not to come to us any more:

> I could see that you really prefer to bring up your child in the American way, and I feel we would have difficulties that I like to avoid. You did not follow my directions at all concerning food and four meals, so you better stick to your American book and do as you like. You will certainly understand that I cannot change my habits for your sake at my age, and I hate working for people who don't agree with me.

I appreciated Katya for her talents and love of her profession. Her training held me in good stead with my next two babies, but it was an unfortunate experience. Sometimes cultural differences matter.

Our biggest shock, the most devastating memory of our lives in Switzerland, happened on November 22, 1963, thirty-six days after Steven was born. President Kennedy was shot and killed in Dallas at 12:30 P.M. With the time difference, we were eating dinner while we watched the German-language television. It was hard to make out exactly what happened. Was he wounded? Who did it? Philippe quickly turned on his short-wave radio. Governor John Connally of Texas was seriously wounded. The president was dead. I was inconsolable. Europe went into mourning for this vibrant young man whose personality had captivated the continent. A White House official mentioned the open limousine in which Kennedy was riding with Governor Connally and their wives: "We had a choice between security and politics, and we chose politics." My letter home reflected our loneliness in not being able to share this loss with family and close friends:

> We're absolutely grief stricken about Kennedy! All we can do is to try to hear the Armed Forces Network or the Voice of America, both of which fade in and out with static from each passing tram. It's maddening. How I wish we could watch this on American television so we could learn what happened. What a waste. What a loss of a brilliant, attractive man. The country won't see his equal in many years. As for Mrs. Kennedy, she practically had no married life to begin with. Then losing her baby, and now her husband. I can tell you, living in Europe, how proud we were that we had such a president and his wife. Now they're gone from public life. I think Lyndon Johnson is a good man, but I have an uneasy feeling that the country is in for rough times on the foreign scene. Maybe Johnson, with his prestige in the Senate, can get more united action. This, plus the effect of the assassination, might get results where Kennedy couldn't. We don't know any reasons. Right now, it's a colossal tragedy. Was it the fault of the Secret Service? What's the difference. We're following the news the best we can.

I was moved to tears at the picture of John-John saluting his father's coffin. I thought at the time that this little boy, son of our fallen leader, could surely be a future U.S. president himself. Fate would have its way, as it often did in the Kennedy family.

30

On Wednesday, November 27th, American residents in Zurich were invited to a memorial service for President Kennedy. The French Reformed Church was jammed both with Americans and Swiss. It was the first time we saw so many Americans together in Zurich. But we were far from home. We had lost our president. We needed each other.

From the capital of Bern, one American wrote a letter to the *New York Times* that although Switzerland was neutral and had no military alliance with or aid from America, due respects were paid to the president. Thousands of people assembled in a torchlight procession and marched in pouring rain to the residence of the American ambassador to express their condolences. Another letter praised Kennedy for making the world safer with a test-ban treaty, strengthening democratic principles in the Cuban crisis, and providing Latin America with new faith in an Alliance for Progress.

President de Gaulle was among the dignitaries at Arlington Cemetery attending Kennedy's funeral. At first, the old general had discouraged the young American president from coming to France to discuss world matters and to share his views as an elder statesman, but when a state visit finally took place in May 1961, de Gaulle seemed quite at ease with Kennedy and his French-speaking, elegant wife, Jacqueline. As warmly as the French public greeted the Kennedys, they now deeply mourned for him, cruelly stricken down in his prime, calling him a defender of all rights and all freedoms. Ironically, the assassination in Dallas reinforced Franco-American friendship, at least for a little while. All of Europe was saddened.

After the grief subsided, Europe's concern was Lyndon Baines Johnson, an unknown quantity. *U.S. News and World Report* wrote, "Harvard is out, the University of Texas is in." Johnson was described as a great Senate majority leader, politically astute, a realist. One Swiss commented that he might not be as brilliant or intellectual as Kennedy, but he gets results. LBJ was determined to "reason together." The swift transition of the presidency to Johnson, who was sworn in aboard Air Force One, returning the presidential party from Texas back to Washington, D.C., was considered in Europe as uniquely American, one of our country's strengths.

One of President Johnson's first acts in late November 1963 was to create a commission to investigate the assassination of President Kennedy under the chairmanship of Chief Justice Earl Warren of the Supreme Court. On September 27, 1964, a summary of the Warren Commission report was released, to be followed by twenty-six volumes of documents, interviews, and depositions. It was hoped that the report would put to rest a conspiracy theory in the minds of the public, then rampant in articles, books, and film.

The lone assassin was identified as Lee Harvey Oswald, an ex-Marine, a loner, who once had defected to the Soviet Union and could not adjust to life in America. The commission noted the failure of the FBI to forward the background information it had about Oswald to the Secret Service in charge of protecting the president. J. Edgar Hoover, the director of the FBI, claimed that since nothing in Oswald's previous history was considered dangerous, there was no need to furnish his name to the Secret Service or the Dallas police. In all of Europe, only the French remained convinced of a conspiracy. Their left-wing newspapers maintained that it was a right-wing plot.

As a diversion from the dreary news, I ran down to Jelmoli when it was celebrating American Week with its motto, "Live Like an American." The department store was jammed. Official figures showed a 20 percent rise in sales above the French products featured the year before, an American triumph. I did my share – two kitchen gadgets and a pot holder.

But in 1964, there was no diversion from the reactions to the civil rights cause and the Vietnam War at home. On June 21, three civil rights, voter-registration volunteers, Michael Schwerner, Andrew Goodman, and James Earl Chaney, were brutally murdered in Mississippi. Congress passed and Lyndon Johnson signed the Civil Rights Act eleven days later on July 2. Congress had been persuaded both by the events and the persuasive skills for which the president was known. The church bombings of the past years and the death of the volunteers were suspected to have been generated by the Ku Klux Klan. In Vietnam fifteen thousand five hundred American troops were slowly shifting from an advisory to a combat role. The cost to the United States was $1.5 million a day. The count of dead and wounded was growing. The GIs felt we did not care. We did. It was just that American support of South Vietnam's unpopular ruler in a civil war with the North did not seem to justify our presence.

In July 1964, Barry Goldwater, a conservative senator from Arizona, became the official Republican candidate for president. The liberal English newspaper *The Guardian* described him as a "sort of Rip Van Winkle who has been asleep since 1776." His state-ment at the party's convention in San Francisco, "Extremism in the defense of liberty is no vice," put Europe on edge. I stood in the kitchen aghast at his speech being broadcast on the radio, "Did you hear what he just said?!" The possible use of nuclear weapons in war by the superpowers, or any country that could acquire such capability, was a shock.

At the end of August, Lyndon Johnson accepted the presidential nomination of his party at the Democratic convention in Atlantic City. He was quick to reassure the public, "We cannot act rashly with the nuclear weapons that could destroy us all." His words were temperate, but it was the Tonkin Gulf incident that already had provided him with congres-sional support to broaden the war in Vietnam. On August 4, North Vietnamese torpedo boats engaged in a second attack on the U.S. destroyers Maddox and Turner Joy in what the president said were international waters. The details were sketchy, but the course was set.

I was determined to get my absentee ballot for the November election immediately, but by chance, I was to vote in America. In September, we took our vacation in Elizabeth, New Jersey, where my mother and stepfather lived. Steven was beginning to walk, our second baby was expected in January, and we all reveled in the warmth of family for a short while. Quite unexpectedly, Philippe had an interview with the investment firm of Wertheim in New York. He was asked to manage its Paris office, and so began studying (successfully) for his principal's exam. The decision was for me to stay in America until the baby was born. Philippe would return to Zurich, wrap things up, and arrange to ship our earthly possessions for the move to France.

Lyndon Johnson won the election overwhelmingly in November 1964, by 486 electoral votes to Goldwater's 52. President Kennedy's New Frontier became President Johnson's Great Society. A month before the election, Red China exploded its first atom bomb. It was just one problem that would plague his years in office.

Vicky, *London Evening Standard,* November 26, 1963

33

The family predictions were that I would have a girl – and so it was. Deborah Ruth was born in mid-January 1965, ten days before her due date. When I finally arranged for Steven's care at home, I was late getting to the hospital. My obstetrician, who had been waiting for me for two hours since my alert call to his office, was beside himself. We were on friendly enough terms for him to blurt out, "Where the hell have you been?" It was an un-Swiss question, but understandable, given the forty-five minutes it took for my daughter to be born.

By March, we were packed and ready to move to Paris. My letters to Philippe in Paris were full of questions. "Can we get Similac over there? Is there fluoride in the water? Has the new apartment got enough closet space or drawers for the children's clothes? And please get the name of a pediatrician right away."

Zurich would soon become a memory, a place of beautiful beginnings. I remembered fondly the conductors of Number 11 tram who patiently lifted my pram and new baby aboard. It was a courtesy expected and approved by the Swiss. No one complained that the delay to board took too much time. There was the friendly butcher two blocks south of our apartment on the Forchstrasse. I had been told by Sister Katya to ask for *"Leber gehackt fini für ein bebe,"* (liver chopped fine for a baby). Raw liver is given to a baby, a real American no-no. In order to spare my having to repeat this phrase each time, the butcher had it ready for me whenever he saw me coming down the street.

The people of Zurich were always kind. Their warm, spontaneous greeting of *Grüezi*, or *Grüezi mitenand* (greetings with another) to both of us, was described by Gene Epstein as "the most important word in Switzerland, the equivalent of hi, neighbor." We heard the best European orchestras, took Steven to the zoo, walked the quaint city streets in the old town on the east side of the Limmat River, and ate well. Visitors were constant. Many friends changed their travel plans to come to Zurich, if only to see how we two former New Yorkers were coping.

There were comfortingly small, well-kept neighborhood parks ideal for an afternoon rest after pushing the baby carriage up the Zurich hills. Frequent downpours never stopped mothers from walking their babies. A white pram cover was quickly installed, the kind with the clear plastic insert at eye level so the baby could peer out. On one of our walks in the woods, Steven began to cry when the loud gunshots of a Swiss militia having firing practice was heard from a nearby range. It was more noise than he could bear. We made a hasty retreat.

To people who told me before I left for Switzerland that I would be bored, I learned quickly that no place is boring when you have a baby to care for. The surroundings, the people, and the scenery were totally conducive to peace of mind. I loved Zurich. It was where my life was at that moment in time.

34

My favorite Swiss festival was the annual *Sechseläuten* (below), which was celebrated in Zurich on the third Sunday and Monday in April in front of the Opera House to commemorate the return of spring, or end of winter, depending on one's mood. It was sheer pageantry to see horsemen in costumes representing the trades of twenty-six guilds of the Middle Ages racing around a giant snowman (the *Böögg*) stuffed with straw and fireworks on a pole. At 6 P.M. (*sechs uhr*), the effigy would be set on fire to the ringing (*läuten*) of vesper bells. The crowd cheered and clapped as the horses ran in a circle at a dizzying pace. It was a challenge to explain to my New York friends that a semi-pagan rite in the atomic age still mesmerized the crowd. And I was one of them.

During my temporary sojourn in New Jersey awaiting the birth of my second child, I was beginning to see the world through a different light. Living in Switzerland, admittedly not what the diplomatic corps would describe as a hardship post, was a useful experience in learning what was necessary to adjust to foreign surroundings. The eleventh commandment was never to criticize the host country and always have something positive to say about it. In Switzerland, it was an easy commandment to observe. My own, my native land of America, which to me was the best of all possible worlds, was inching toward foreign entanglements. The founding fathers would not have recognized this superpower now involved with stopping the spread of communism on the Asian continent.

The Swiss had a different way of dealing with their absolute conviction of being the best country on the planet – restricting citizenship. One acquaintance of ours who had been in the country for ten years without having been granted the privilege, called it "their pride in the Swiss passport." Having been born in Zurich, Steven did not automatically become Swiss. His American passport, secured within a week of his birth, confirmed his nationality. Whatever his destiny might be, it would not include guarding an Alp.

Although content with its seemingly perfect life, Swiss drivers were not immune from being ticketed for speeding, possibly a release from the controlled behavior demanded by such perfection and the unrelenting rules of the road. A local problem in Zurich was the growing drug culture of users and dealers from all parts of Europe taking place behind the Bahnhof. Addicted, disheveled youths spent their time in that area where their friends gathered daily to accommodate their habit. It took a while for a city crackdown to take place.

The one negative that we had heard about Switzerland was the official government policy during World War II of turning back thousands of Jewish refugees attempting to enter this neutral country after fleeing Nazi Germany or the surrounding occupied lands of Austria, France, and Belgium, usually to face certain death. Swiss border guards, directed by Heinrich Rothmond, Bern's chief of police, who feared an inundation of foreigners, gave the unfortunate Jews no quarter. This, in the country whose tradition is one of political asylum, home of the Red Cross, founded by the humanitarian, Henri Dunant. But the Jews were considered racial, not political, refugees.

German tourists did not require a visa to enter Switzerland, so in order to stem the refugee tide, it was by Rothmond's initiative that the red *J* for *Jude,* or Jew, came to be stamped on the passports of German or Austrian Jews. The Nazis later adopted this practice of the red *J* on the passports of all Jews in Germany and in countries that they occupied. The Swiss Jewish community was required to pay upkeep for the twenty-five thousand refugees whom the government previously had allowed in. In Swiss financial dealings, the tendency was to placate Germany, whose economy was important to Switzerland and whose bankers continued to do business with the Nazis. In this respect, Swiss neutrality did not apply.

The border police, however, were no reflection of the people themselves. According to Alfred Häsler in his book, *The Lifeboat is Full,* the Swiss, steeped in democratic principles and its country's right of asylum, inundated officials in Bern with letters and telegrams of protest about the treatment of Jewish refugees. His stories of valor included a Swiss nurse in Zurich who, in Christian charity, filled every room of her father's house with refugees, and a child selling Zwingli calendars for five francs apiece who turned over the money to a refugee fund. Diplomats also were among those who felt it was their duty to help Jewish refugees facing extinction during World War II. The most vocal in criticizing the government were members of the Swiss clergy, claiming that human decency had been abandoned.

Another specific example of humanity was Paul Grüninger, the police chief of St. Gallen canton on the Austrian border, who falsified entry documents in order to save three thousand Jews fleeing Nazi persecution in 1938-39. For disobeying orders and jeopardizing Switzerland's official neutrality, he was arrested, fined, and convicted by the Swiss authorities. His salary and pension were terminated, and he was reduced to near poverty.

The Swiss Red Cross, reacting to the fate of families from neighboring countries caught in the worst personal crisis of the twentieth century, saved many Jewish children through the humanitarian efforts of its Children's Support Program. In those dark, dismal days, the conscience of the Swiss was a beacon of light.

During our eighteen months in Zurich, a memory remains of Switzerland's peaceful, natural beauty. One cold, predawn morning in November 1963, I awoke, unable to sleep, anticipating the first rustlings of my one-month-old infant to start my day. A full moon reflected on the lake of Zurich, which we clearly could see from our apartment. It still was too dark to distinguish the trees below. Suddenly, from the north there came far-off cries of honking snow geese. They were flying south in V-formation silhouetted against the moon. The world was quiet except for their echoes floating off into the sky. I stepped onto the balcony to watch them fly until they were out of sight. In the quickening dawn, the trees were beginning to take form, and the lights from the houses on the opposite side of the lake slowly increased with the start of another workday. Total silence. Then the baby woke. The sights and sounds of the new day were filled with the memory of migrating snow geese and the needs of a hungry baby. Life in Switzerland made few other demands.

In total contrast, Neuilly, the nearest suburb west of Paris, city of marvelous light, was to become our home in March 1965. France, at the heart of history, revolution, and conflict for centuries, now was staking her claim to a postwar place in the sun under the leadership of the indomitable Charles de Gaulle. We were about to trade a traditionally neutral country for one of strong political opinions. Anti-Americanism was increasing as de Gaulle was determined to achieve French independence from American influence, particularly with his opposition to the Vietnam War. Tensions between the two countries heightened. For de Gaulle, the grandeur of France was alive and well.

After a trip to the customs office on Battery Place in New York City to fill out the proper documents, I labeled the trunks filled with baby clothes and essentials and waited for them to be picked up in New Jersey and delivered to the next ship sailing for France. Our furniture and belongings were already in France, thanks to Philippe's diligent arrangements while in Zurich. My last letter to him in Paris ended: "Here goes nothing."

At Orly airport near midnight, holding Steven's hand and Debby wrapped in her plaid blanket, I met Philippe after a three-month family hiatus, exhausted but excited to start the French chapter of our lives.

38

[II]
NEUILLY - sur - SEINE

In a tranquil, tree-shaded garden behind the city hall, the Hôtel de Ville, facing our apartment on the boulevard Jean Mermoz, neighborhood children from different lands and languages mingled with their French playmates in peaceful coexistence. A long, oval sandbox for the toddlers, who arrived daily with pail and shovel, was an inspired consideration of the city planners. A bust of Jean Mermoz (1901-1936), for whom the boulevard was named, still stands in the garden, a tribute to the heroic, ill-fated, young aviator who opened the first, direct postal connection from France to South America and pioneered the Brazil to Chile air route. He disappeared in his hydroplane, the Southern Cross *(Croix du Sud),* off the Atlantic coast of Africa.

40

> "Neuilly! Charming sojourn, sad and sweet memory,
> childhood illusions that never depart."
>
> ALFRED DE MUSSET

A frequent visitor to Neuilly, Musset, the nineteenth-century French poet, perfectly described the city that was to be our home for four years. Our "charming sojourn" and "sweet memory" began in the spring of 1965 when I joined Philippe in France with eighteen-month-old Steven, and three-month-old Debby, whom he had not yet seen. In the sixties, Neuilly was a city of eighty thousand people, an oasis of calm, with wide, tree-lined boulevards, once home to French nobles and literati, who preferred its purer air and suburban tranquility to that of central Paris. Philippe had chosen well.

The flat terrain of Neuilly, unlike the hills of Zurich, was perfect for pushing the baby stroller or wheeling a full shopping cart, the *chariot*, home from the twice-a-week, open-air market or from Monoprix, the well-stocked department store and supermarket, both on the avenue de Neuilly. Across the street from Monoprix, the post office had public telephones that worked erratically during France's frequent strikes.

Along that same major avenue runs metro Line Number 1, which Philippe took daily for his fifteen-minute commute to his office on the place de la Concorde. Returning in the evening to the Sablon stop, he had only a short walk to the boulevard Jean Mermoz, where his eager family was full of stories of the day's events.

Official business was conducted in the imposing Hôtel de Ville, or *mairie,* inaugurated in January 1886. Achille Peretti, who had been the mayor of Neuilly since 1947, was a man of many projects, formerly in the Resistance, and an active fighter in 1944 for the liberation of Paris. It was in the garden square behind the building, which we pronounced in French, the "sqwahr," that one unforgettable day a year later, our independent, fifteen-month-old Debby, playing in the sandbox, calmly took her pail of sand and, for no apparent reason, dumped it on the head of a little boy sitting three feet away. With copious apologies to the shocked mother and gritty-haired, bawling child, we gathered our toys and left quickly for an unexpectedly early lunch and a firm lecture on sandbox etiquette.

On weekends, we walked to the Bois de Boulogne where the children played in what seemed to be endless woods. We had heard that the Duke and Duchess of Windsor had luxurious digs on the grand boulevard facing the Bois. We never knew exactly where, but it was nice to know that royalty appreciated Neuilly as we did.

Another celebrity, the adventurous aviator, Jean Mermoz, who was immortalized on his pedestal in the city hall square, had lost his life at the age of thirty-five. He had assigned the Patagonia flight route to another famous but unfortunate pilot, Antoine Saint-Exupéry, whose plane disappeared in July 1944 on a reconnaissance mission from Corsica over occupied France. (Sixty years later, it was found and dredged up from the Mediterranean Sea off the coast of Marseilles.) Saint-Exupéry left us his masterpiece, *Le Petit Prince,* about a golden-haired boy from a tiny planet who needed a friend. I would read it to Steven and Debby after their dinner and bath. What was the meaning of the secret that the fox told to the Little Prince? – "But eyes are blind. You must look with the heart." We talked about that – what is important is not what you see but what you feel – in terms they could understand. Then it was time for bed.

In front and atop the Hôtel de Ville, a large decorative clock reminds passersby that "It is the hour to do good." One who did good was Antoine-Augustin Parmentier, an agronomist and economist, who planted the first potato seeds as an experiment in the Sablon plain in Neuilly in 1786. His statue (right) in front of the Hôtel de Ville shows a serious Parmentier, with his hoe at his feet, gazing at a potato. Louis XVI favored the new, starchy tuber by serving it at his dinner table. The statue was the least Neuilly could do to honor the man who enabled one of France's culinary traditions, the *pomme frite,* the venerable French fry.

On the western side of the building, we often saw immigrant workers from Africa, waiting silently, stoically, with their brooms for their daily street-sweeping assignments. If there was no work, their sole source of income, it might have been a sad day without pay.

42

The streets of Neuilly recalled other once-famous residents. We shopped for basic necessities on the next street, rue de Chezy, named for the engineer, Antoine de Chezy, who directed the construction of the bridge, the Pont de Neuilly, at the western edge of the city in the eighteenth century. Steven saw his first movie, *Dr. Doolittle,* in the small movie house now called the Village on rue de Chezy. At four years of age, as the picture started, he suddenly called out, "Where did the lights go?" to the annoyance of an elderly couple, the only other ones in the theater at the time. The Cours Montaigne, where the children attended school, was on the rue Charles Laffitte, named for a nineteenth-century financier and overseer of the extensive land in the Bois de Boulogne. The street leading to the metro on the avenue de Neuilly was named for Louis Philippe, who lived in Neuilly with his family before being named "citizen king" in 1830. Other street names honored mayors, generals, artists, doctors, engineers, painters, members of the Resistance, a priest, and even one unfortunate man who was guillotined. As head of France's provisional government in 1945-46, Charles de Gaulle moved to a house in Neuilly, which his wife, Yvonne, described as "rather better than what I would have liked." De Gaulle considered it appropriate to his position.

Historically, Neuilly was known for its excellent laundry facilities. Napoleon's sister, Pauline Borghese, a town resident (with the right connections), had the river banks cleared of stagnant waters to assure that fine linens and garments could be washed without risk of infection from insects. At her behest, Napoleon had his wash sent to Neuilly. In the best Neuilly tradition, our good *blanchisserie* off the rue de Chezy on rue Perronet – Rodolphe Perronet constructed the Neuilly bridge with Antoine Chezy – did fine work at reasonable prices, thus sparing us from struggling weekly to launder king-size sheets, pillowcases and tablecloths in a small washing machine that only could fit into a French apartment. When one of our pillowcases got lost, the apologetic owner gave us a yellow embroidered table-cloth with six matching napkins. It was a generous exchange that we remember fondly from the "unfriendly" French.

Some other industries that once thrived in Neuilly included lace-trimming; weaving; knitting; perfumeries with their assorted aromatic products; automobile construction and repair shops; and marble from the quarries on the Ile de la Jatte, the island to the west on the Seine.

An important feature of Neuilly was the American Hospital, our refuge for unexpected mishaps, such as a broken finger, clavicle, or cuts that needed stitches. "Here come the Feyericks again," was our greeting as we arrived in the emergency room with whichever child needed attention. It was on the maternity floor of the hospital that my third child, Andrew, was born in 1969, a month before we planned to pack our things and return to America.

This expansive facility on the boulevard Victor Hugo was inaugurated as a twenty-four-bed hospital in 1909 by Americans, but not solely for Americans. During both world wars, the American Hospital was a vital factor in caring for Allied wounded as well as civilians. In the sixties, the new Eisenhower wing was finished, which included a nuclear medicine service. Many a French dignitary and executive sought the hospital for care, even while denying that it was any better than a French facility in Paris. On one of my many visits to the hospital, Brigitte Bardot, the French actress, was just entering. Even as a semi-incognito presence, she was worthy of her fame. Due to our proximity to the hospital, we were tied into its electrical grid and were sometimes spared the blackouts or refrigerator spoilage that plagued Paris during labor strikes.

Another historic American connection to Neuilly was the Lycée Pasteur on the boulevard d'Inkermann, now a boys prestigious secondary school. During World War I, it was home base to American ambulances since a five-hundred-bed hospital had been set up for casualties. We used to walk past it on summer days when the children wanted to swim at the covered pool of the sports complex, a project of the popular Mayor Peretti. A portion of the commercial avenue du Roule now bears his name. The lycée was named for the microbiologist, Louis Pasteur, whose method of destroying microorganisms in liquids revolutionized the safety of milk, milk products, and beer. In the heart of Pasteur land, I would ask the milk seller at the open market for pasteurized milk or cheese. Her answer, probably because she had none to sell, was, "You don't know what real milk tastes like." I was not about to risk it.

On our daily walk to the Cours Montaigne school, we passed the synagogue on the corner of rue Ancelle and rue Jacques Dulud. Constructed in 1878 for the growing number of Jews coming from Alsace and Lorraine, it had its own story to tell. The most pitiful was that of the Nazi roundup of thousands of French Jews at the Vélodrome d'Hiver in July 1942, their deportation to the Drancy internment camp, and their final extermination at Auschwitz. The rabbi of the Neuilly synagogue, Robert Meyers, and his wife were among those who lost their lives. The synagogue itself was saved.

In the summer of 1966, we saw two moving men carrying an enormous pool table into the downstairs apartment. The next week, the D'Gerolamos arrived. John was an IBM executive. His wife, the unflappable Joan, with her Louisiana southern accent, faced life unafraid, like moving to Paris with four children and little knowledge of French. The oldest, Steve, thirteen years old, bright and quiet like John, was known as "big" Steve in contrast to my "little" Steve; next was Diane, ten years old, serious and shy, with the obvious capability of her mother; then Mark, a handsome eight-year-old; and the youngest, two-and-a-half-year-old Matthew, closer to Debby's age and often her afternoon playmate after nap time when Steven was at the Cours Montaigne. The first three attended the American School of Paris, first in Louvecienne and later in Saint-Cloud, going and returning by bus every school day. The treat of the week for Debby and Steven was a standing invitation downstairs each Thursday afternoon to see *Jeudimage,* the French equivalent of *Sesame Street.* We shared Thanksgiving together, when the pool table was transformed into a help-yourself buffet laden with Joan's bountiful, traditional American meal. At Christmas, Steven thought that the D'Gerolamo's brightly decorated tree was "a really big Hanukah bush."

I admired Joan's assured, non-verbal way of shopping at the Neuilly open market. The French merchants bowed to her every wish. Her pointing finger had a Ph.D. in home economics, a tribute to her professional background as a dietician. When she saw a certain piece of fish, cheese, or fruit, she pointed. *"Ça!"* (that one). *"Ça?"* asked the merchant. "No," she said. Then the finger pointed again, and the one she wanted was selected, paid for, and placed triumphantly into her shopping bag. Joan was determined to get the best out of France, like improving on her already superb cooking. The most difficult French dishes to master, like the delicate fish dish, *quenelles de brochet,* became second nature to her. She also attempted to take French in a class for Americans near the IBM office. She entered with a hearty "Bonjour, y'all." Everyone perked up, "Here's Joan."

Our mutual favorite, called by Joan "the little man," was a serious functionary who rang the doorbell monthly to dole out the *allocations familiales,* the government family allowance check, from his leather pouch – the more children, the bigger the amount. Foreign families paying taxes in France also were entitled to receive the allowance. "The little man" was a welcome sight.

Since 1939, the government initiated family subsidy legislation due to the falling birthrate in France. The population had been decimated in two world wars. In World War I alone, François Nourissier in his book, *The French,* called the 1.35 million war dead, with an additional 2.5 million casualties and war widows, "a hemorrhage that bled France white." In 1945, Charles De Gaulle, as head of the provisional government, stated his wish to see "twelve million beautiful babies for France in the next ten years." As president in 1967, de Gaulle backed further legislation with the aim of improving France's living standards and hopefully boosting her birthrate. The monthly checks resulted in a rise of eight hundred thousand births annually. In the sixties, France's low birthrate was now the highest in Europe and its population the youngest.

We joined French families on weekends crowding into one of Neuilly's major attractions, the Jardin d'Acclimatation in the Bois de Boulogne, a facility inaugurated in 1860 by Napoleon III. Children eagerly lined up for the kiddie rides and the decorated carousel. Small, white plastic ovals stamped with the names of the rides were the entrance tickets to each up-and-down, or round-and-round, two-minute amusement. Separated from the strolling crowds by a watery moat, a brown polar bear paced endlessly on his rocky perch. We sometimes went together with the D'Gerolamo children to the hall of crazy mirrors where the distorted fat, thin, shortened, or elongated young bodies sent them into gales of laughter. A boat ride, which wound around a short water course with a churning water wheel at the end, topped a pleasant Sunday afternoon.

Jardin d'Acclimatation, fall 1967

We delighted in the children as they began to speak French, learned from their playmates in the square and later at school, combined with English, as we spoke it at home. Their half-and-half sentences – Open the *porte* (door); *Donne* (give) the ball; *Où est* (where is) the car?; You are *méchant* (naughty) – were often hilarious but also a lesson in how young minds adapt deftly to languages. Much to Philippe's secret delight, his mother tongue was in the ascendance, and I had two children who would keep my French current in daily conversation.

46

[III]
CHARLES DE GAULLE

CHARLES DE GAULLE REGNANTE (1958.1965)

Moisan, *Le Canard Enchâiné*, December 1, 1965

LE PRÉSIDENT

So here we were in France. I never knew the name of the head of the Swiss government when we lived in Zurich. Life in a neutral country was relatively idyllic, no need to fret about politics. But there was no mistaking the French president, the dauntless Charles de Gaulle, who was elected in 1958, and whose successful reelection in December 1965 guaranteed him another seven years in office. In a country of nine political parties and an independent-minded electorate, this was no small accomplishment.

In the sixties, President de Gaulle, a former general and leader of the Free French in exile during World War II, was determined to regain France's place as an international player and to revive her past grandeur *(la gloire de la France)*. His dual motives were Europe for the Europeans from "the Atlantic to the Urals" and maintaining neutrality between the two major powers, America and the Soviet Union. National rivalries seemed to be more between our old ally France and the United States than the United States and the Soviet Union, our principal antagonist in the ongoing cold war.

De Gaulle's dealings with the American and British Allies had not been ideal during the Second World War when he headed the Free French operations in London. At first, President Roosevelt refused to recognize de Gaulle's National Committee of Liberation as the representative of France, maintaining instead diplomatic ties in 1940 with the free zone, or Vichy France, headed by Marshal Philippe Pétain. De Gaulle saw in Roosevelt an "Anglo-Saxon tendency to dominate," while England to him was a nation with "a ruthless love of power," even though Prime Minister Winston Churchill gave the general access to communications so that he could keep in contact with the remnants of his Free French fighting forces in Europe and Africa. Their mutual colonial interests in Africa and the Middle East were bound to conflict. In 1942, after a difficult meeting with de Gaulle, Churchill stated his famous complaint, referring to the adopted symbol of the Free French, "We all have our crosses to bear. Mine is the Cross of Lorraine."

OPPOSITE PAGE: The trappings of monarchy adorn the French president, satirized here as Louis XIV, as inspired by the *Memoirs of the Duc de Saint-Simon,* written by a statesman in the sun king's royal court. Among the king's attributes were those applicable to President de Gaulle – courage, love of glory, and a court filled with illustrious and clever men. De Gaulle's "clever men" (below) include Prime Minister Georges Pompidou (left); Finance Minister Valéry Giscard d'Estaing (center) seen as a sharp-eared hawk; and Minister of Culture André Malraux (right foreground) dressed as a museum guard. Strange animals creep around the royal feet, possibly signifying needy petitioners. Above the monarch's head fly two Gaullist ministers as winged angels, one bestowing a kingly wreath. An atom bomb (far right) represents de Gaulle's *force de frappe,* his nuclear strike force, intended to insure France's security against foreign attack.

According to General de Gaulle's memoir *Unity* that recounted World War II events from 1942 to 1944, he was convinced that President Roosevelt was doing everything he could to prevent France from regaining power in continental Europe. While he admired General Dwight Eisenhower, then the supreme commander of the Allied Expeditionary Force, de Gaulle was determined to block Roosevelt's intention of having Eisenhower take charge of the administration of France. A disgruntled de Gaulle would write, "I could defy General Eisenhower to deal lawfully with anyone I had not designated." The French generals Pierre Koenig and Jacques Leclerc, who had been assigned by de Gaulle to Allied commands, were only on loan and not bound by any orders but his. When de Gaulle visited Washington, D.C., on July 6, 1944, he realized that Roosevelt believed France's defeat disqualified her from decision making on the same level as the Big Four: Great Britain, the U.S., China, and the Soviet Union. Some years later, de Gaulle remarked, "If I had not been here, France would already have fallen completely into the hands of America, there's no question about that."

We remembered the 6-foot-5-inch figure of General de Gaulle in Paris on August 26, 1944, walking at the head of the victory procession from the Etoile down the Champs Elysées with other military luminaries behind him. De Gaulle had decided that only Frenchmen, not the Allies, should participate in order to give the French a sense of renewal and pride. His main concern was a possible clash with the French Communists who played a great part in the Resistance and who were anxious to seize power and form a de facto government before de Gaulle had the chance to do so. But his visit to the Prefecture of Police the day before the parade insured that he would have support in case of trouble. Four years of German occupation were over. The Vichy regime was finished. On that great day of victory, General de Gaulle felt that he was "an instrument of destiny," even as he told the notables in the procession, "Messieurs, one step behind me."

With the defeat of France's army at Dien Bien Phu in 1954 at the hands of Communist Vietminh forces and its withdrawal from French Indochina, American troops in the sixties began to fill the vacuum. President De Gaulle warned the U.S. against getting involved in this "dirty war," as he had previously advised his wartime ally Dwight Eisenhower, then also his nation's president, on a visit to Camp David in 1960, that despite America's importance, he did not wish to see it act as universal judge and policeman.

De Gaulle also opted to form a Franco-German alliance and encourage détente with the Soviets and Eastern European countries. This would allow NATO to reduce its forces in Europe, which were on alert to contain communism. According to John Hess in *The Case for De Gaulle,* such a move would allow the rival superpowers to focus instead on alleviating world poverty. Hess found de Gaulle to be prophetic but added, "I'm afraid we shall never forgive him for it."

One morning in March 1966, a year after we arrived in Paris, we heard President de Gaulle declare on the radio that NATO, based in Fontainebleau and Versailles, and SHAPE (Supreme Headquarters Allied Powers in Europe), in Rocquencourt outside of Paris had one year to leave France. He felt that geographically France was too vulnerable to a direct Soviet attack to be dependent on a U.S.-dominated NATO for her security, and that in this atomic age it was imperative for a great nation to have its own nuclear capability, his *force de frappe,* to defend itself. France already had exploded her first atomic bomb at a testing ground in Algeria on February 13, 1960. In any confrontation with the Soviets, Europe again could become an unwilling battleground. By expelling foreign forces from her soil, it would prove to the Soviets that France did not rely on America for her safety. As of July 1, French troops in Germany would cease to be under NATO command.

.. JE NE JOUE PLUS NA !..

De Gaulle to NATO: "I won't play with you any more!"
J. Lap. *Combat,* June 3, 1965.

Two days before the April 1,1967 deadline, NATO and SHAPE Allied military installations left France for Belgium. After sixteen years, the flags were lowered. The British military band played "Charlie Is My Darling," described by the *New Yorker*'s Janet Flanner in her *Paris Journal* as "the wittiest, most sarcastic musical rebuke possible" to President "Charlie" de Gaulle. According to statistics, thirty thousand troops and airmen and thirty-five thousand dependents left French soil, along with eight hundred twenty thousand tons of materiel. In Rocquencourt and Fontainebleu there was less joy in seeing France's military allies depart. Many appreciated their friendliness and local patronage. With the troops gone, the cost to the French economy was $200 million a year.

My Belgian father-in-law, basically pro-American, had mixed emotions. Proud as he was that his country was chosen and agreed to host the incoming military defense organizations and their personnel, he felt it was the end of an era. The longtime, faithful help so indispensable in running large Belgian households now might be lured away by the higher pay offered by the newly arriving families, especially the Americans. Such are the personal dilemmas of international politics.

In much appreciated and rare pro-American editorials in the popular daily newspaper, *Le Figaro,* André François-Poncet, the former French ambassador to West Germany and member of the Académie française, wrote that telling NATO and SHAPE to leave France was a serious error, which he deplored. He reminded readers that France originally had asked the Americans to install their military base here for the defense of the free world. Being part of these combined military efforts in no way reduced France to a state of dependence on America. Their current departure "will never free us of the debt we owe the country that saved our lives." It was ungrateful of France to carry on such an anti-American campaign, and he hoped that when things changed (probably post-de Gaulle), the chasm between the two countries would not deepen further. He concluded, "This is my wish and the wish of thousands of Frenchmen."

Regardless of our reaction to the French declaration to withdraw from NATO, de Gaulle's biographer, Bernard Ledwidge, wrote, "He was no more anti-American than he was pro-Russian," and to his credit was "the first to call for an end to the policy of the rival blocs." To his foreign minister, de Gaulle explained his shock-value behavior, "Monsieur le Ministre, a nation worthy of the name has no friends."

Art Buchwald, writing in the *International Herald Tribune,* satirized the situation in his column, "Handling De Gaulle." The French president expected us to react in rage and disbelief every time he made a statement or held a press conference. Buchwald advised our secretary of defense to say: "The Joint Chiefs of Staff do not believe that France has any strategic value in defending Europe and that she should remove herself from NATO." De Gaulle would then insist on belonging to NATO to spite the Joint Chiefs.

Nevertheless, President de Gaulle's actions aggravated relations with Washington. In January 1964, France had recognized Mao Tse-tung's Communist China, a move seen by America as aiding the North Vietnamese enemy backed by China. Washington was convinced that the neutrality proposed by de Gaulle, in which neither China nor the U.S. were to be involved in Vietnam, would lead to a Communist takeover of Southeast Asia, the controversial "domino theory." Now that NATO and SHAPE were gone from France, President de Gaulle believed that the Soviets would be sufficiently convinced of France's independence from Washington to coordinate policy decisions on their own.

If agreement also could be reached on German unification, which de Gaulle favored, Europe would be free of American troops and influence. To encourage détente with the Soviet Union, France initiated state visits to Moscow and cultural exchanges between both countries.

Moisan. *Le Canard Enchâiné,* June 22, 1966

As Peter the Great came to Paris to seek an alliance with France in 1717, so Charles de Gaulle visited Moscow in 1966 to discuss matters of mutual benefit. De Gaulle is shown in Louis XIV style, in keeping with the *Memoirs of the Duc de Saint-Simon,* as a king on horseback with his long, brown wig flowing. In front of the onion-domed St. Basil's Cathedral in Red Square, he is followed by Madame de Gaulle, carried in a sedan chair by cabinet members in plumed hats. They are welcomed by Soviet leaders in business suits – a prone Nikita Khrushchev, with hand outstretched in greeting; Leonid Brezhnev, tipping his hat to his guests; a gaunt Alexei Kosygin between them; and a dapper Andrei Gromyko standing behind various generals. Lenin's statue (right) in front of the Kremlin walls and the Tomb of the Unknown Soldier, warns the French, "Go home." In the sky are a devil-like Lyndon Johnson with pitchfork (left) and his stoic, political adversary, Mao Tse-tung, seated by the clock tower. A parade watcher (right foreground) comments that both the French and Russian revolutions have retained vestiges of the past.

During the sixties, a supranational climate was growing in Europe. Created by the Treaty of Rome in March 1957, the European Economic Community (the EEC), also known as the Common Market, consisted of six countries: France, Italy, West Germany, Belgium, Luxembourg, and Holland. Another of de Gaulle's issues was keeping Great Britain out of the EEC, claiming that its chronic balance of payments deficit and consequent need for a free market flow of products, rather than the tariffs determined by the six EEC members, would wreck that organization. According to de Gaulle, Britain was not even a European country and could not have it all its own way by demanding terms in a European economic union. Ironically, some felt that by coaxing and bullying, France had managed to take the leadership role in the Common Market. In 1965, de Gaulle had threatened a boycott until he secured favorable terms on agricultural subsidies. Two years later, he threatened again, this time to break up the Common Market if the other five nations insisted on supporting Great Britain's entry.

Regarding France's veto of Great Britain joining the Common Market, Art Buchwald had another suggestion on "handling" de Gaulle: We should indicate that America's greatest fear was that France would allow Great Britain into the EEC. "When de Gaulle hears this he will immediately make the British a partner behind our backs." He concluded, "It was a cruel plot but worth a try."

"The Europe of My Six: That is the French Solution"
J. Lap. *Le Canard Enchainé,* July 7, 1965.

The French reaction to de Gaulle's seeming anti-Americanism, as well as to his familiar posturing, was mixed. In view of the political stability that he had brought to France, his "me or chaos" mantra was enough to keep him in office from 1958 to 1969, one of the longest elected terms for a French leader. De Gaulle might speak of renewed grandeur, but the people realized that France was no longer a primary power. One French writer remarked, "De Gaulle doesn't exist. He is just the idea the French have about themselves."

Having been invited to Canadian Expo '67 to celebrate Canada's centennial, de Gaulle took the opportunity on July 24 of that year to address the crowds in Montreal from the balcony of the city hall. He concluded his French oration in a patriotic outburst, translated as "Long live free Quebec," the slogan of Quebec separatists who were aligned against the federal government. Prime Minister Lester Pearson described his statement as unacceptable: "All Canadians are free and don't need to be liberated by General de Gaulle." The rest of the tour was canceled. De Gaulle returned home to face bad reviews in the French press. The newspaper *Le Monde* wrote that he must have known the effect of his words. It was "one of those oratorical escalations of which he is past master."

With de Gaulle's main focus on the international scene, France's growing internal discontents were neglected, including her standard of living, industrial working conditions, low pay, and antiquated educational facilities. Periodic strikes were frequent. In March 1966, the same month that NATO and SHAPE were notified to remove their operations from France, there was a gas and electric strike. We had no electricity, the refrigerator went off, and there was no hot water. Somehow our gas stove still worked. I was bringing pots of hot water into the bathroom so Philippe could bathe and shave. My only comment in my letter home: "It's revolting." It was something that we would have to get used to. The major strikes, *les grèves,* that paralyzed Paris during the Days of May in 1968 threatened to tear the city apart and bring down the government.

In June 1968, still reeling from the May strikes, the French came to realize the need for NATO in Europe when Soviet troops invaded Czechoslovakia in order to squelch uprisings of the liberal forces longing for freedom behind the Iron Curtain. Persistent American talk about cutting U.S. troops in Europe was considered rash by cooler heads. James Reston of the *New York Times* warned that reducing our military would not only abandon our NATO allies and the hopes of oppressed Soviet bloc countries, but also leave Moscow free to "terrorize Western Europe." Such a military reduction, he added, would hinder U.S. access to its nuclear arsenal if a military crisis ever occurred. The French Communist Party, hopeful of gaining strength after the strikes, was seriously embarrassed by the Soviet invasion. De Gaulle was disappointed. He had expected better "from the great Russian people" but was determined to diminish the threat of two rival blocs in Europe and to work for "the liberty of man."

Although détente was his goal, de Gaulle did not enter naively into his dealings with the Soviets. He had experienced Soviet aggression firsthand in 1919 as a captain in the French army on assignment to the military mission in Poland to help the new republic build up its armed forces. The Soviet armies to the east engaged in sporadic conflicts intent on making Poland a Russian satellite. A year later, as the Russians advanced on Warsaw, de Gaulle saw action as a battalion commander. The Poles counterattacked. The Russians retreated. (It was not until September 17, 1939, that the Soviet army entered Poland sixteen days after the German invasion that officially began World War II. Poland was carved up between Russia and Germany.)

After he returned from Poland, Captain de Gaulle was appointed assistant professor of history at Saint-Cyr military academy. A natural leader with a statesman's perspective, de Gaulle told his students, "People get the history they deserve." Forty years later, however, after the Soviets entered Czechoslovakia, his disappointment with "the great Russian people" recognized that the repression imposed on them by their Communist leaders left them with no choice. His comment to his class at Saint-Cyr, "There are moments when the will of a handful of free men breaks through determinism and opens up new roads," was a prediction of the growing discontent of the countries within the Soviet orbit, as evidenced by Czechoslovakia in 1968. To those students who feared the inevitability of Soviet dominance, de Gaulle warned that such a defeatist attitude was "worse than stupidity," and a "sin against the Holy Spirit."

In 1968, after ten years as president of France, despite the new Soviet assault, de Gaulle continued to seek rapprochement between the Eastern and Western blocs. He had only one year left in office to see if it could be achieved.

[IV]
THE FRENCH

— *Oui, Maggy est à Paris pour apprendre le français.*

Morez. *Paris Match,* Oct. 13, 1962

Anti-Americanism in France was the tone of the sixties due to President de Gaulle's determination to separate his policies from those of the United States and his vehement opposition to the Vietnam War. Yet this did not stop the infiltration of Anglo-Saxon words into the French language. English phrases were running rampant in daily French usage, much to the dismay of the Académie française, a group of forty "immortals," a chosen elite who are the watchdogs of linguistic purity. I did *le shopping* daily, and for the children's birthdays took them to *le Drugstore* for *un sandwich* and *un milkshake*. After lunch, if there was time, we might look for *les blue jeans* or *les pullovers*.

The aim of the Académie, founded in 1635 by Cardinal Richelieu during the reign of Louis XIII, was to provide the country with one unifying language, as opposed to the dialects used in different parts of France. The great fear during the sixties was that foreign language imports would forfeit France's character as a nation and her traditional place as a world cultural leader. It was studiously ignored that English was the current lingua franca in most areas of international relations. To the academicians who monitored the French language, this was trench warfare. Attention had to be paid.

A Sorbonne professor of comparative literature, René Etiemble, railed against *franglais*, a combination of *français*, French, and *anglais*, English. He complained, "At the current rate of corruption there won't be any French language left in forty years. We'll be speaking a transatlantic gibberish that I call *franglais*." Etiemble later was to trace the rising trend in his book *Parlez-vous franglais?* It began slowly in the eighteenth century with words like "drawing room," "roast beef," and "toast." With British power ascending in the nineteenth century after Napoleon's final defeat at Waterloo in 1815, English words in France increased, such as "lunch," "touring," "boarding house," and "high life." In the twentieth century, as France was allied to the Anglo-Saxons in two world wars, with the Free French based in London learning such military terms as "jeep," "half-track," and "commando," and with SHAPE and NATO in France, the barrage of English words reached mega-proportions. After World War II, as American businessmen and tourists began to flood into Paris, English signs appeared in railroad stations, airports, and public places. American publicity, with words like "thrilling," "ultramodern," "streamlined," and its appeal to French youth, did the rest.

OPPOSITE PAGE: Signs in English shown here along the Champs-Elysées seem to contradict the purpose of the girl in pigtails, as her visiting American mother explains to a friend, "Yes, Maggy is in Paris to learn French." Purists considered the infiltration of such foreign words to be the downfall of France's reputation for universal refinement.

Etiemble identified five thousand English or English-sounding words and phrases in French usage. Even in *Le Petit Larousse,* the French dictionary of choice, "quick-freezing," "battle dress," and "discount" appeared. It was a scandal! He offered various suggestions to stop the invasion: The counterattack should begin in nursery school and continue to the upper grades with children learning and loving French through beautiful prose and poetry; radio and television announcers who used *franglais* should pay a penalty; Anglo-Saxon words should be eliminated in French newspapers; merchants who used words like "shopping," or "self-service," should be subject to a heavy tax; all publicity posters should be in French.

The *International Herald Tribune* took Etiemble to task, stating that his attempts to defend the French language should be treated with contempt for wanting it as it was in the time of the seventeenth-century aristocrat, Madame de Sévigné, famous for her letters written in flawless French to her daughter in Provence. But the invasion continued, along with the French craze for American entertainment – the comedian Jerry Lewis, the actor Charles Bronson, 007 movies, and the American style of the French-born rock star Johnny Hallyday.

It was fascinating to discover that French characteristics went as far back as Roman times. In 52 B.C., Julius Caesar faced the tribes of Gaul led by the formidable warrior chief, Vercingetorix, at the siege of Alesia. The Gauls were known to be enthusiastic but undisciplined, unable to stay unified, and treacherous in their shifting alliances. In modern times, the playwright and poet Jean Cocteau thought the French resembled ill-tempered Italians. We once saw a father in the park boot his young son in the rear for misbehaving, and the chef at the Cordon Bleu cooking class whack his assistant with the mixing spoon he needed for his delicate soufflé, which had not been given to him quickly enough. Then there was the irate driver who cut ahead of me in line at the gas pump during one of France's frequent strikes. But these were isolated incidents.

Since personal contacts with the French or invitations to their households were almost nonexistent, our observations were random. François Nourissier in his book *The French* confirmed, "In Paris you can live for twenty years in an apartment house in a good residential area and never become acquainted with, and even scarcely speak to a neighbor you meet regularly in the elevator or on the stairs." He compared it to America and Italy where "first names and familiar forms of address crop up in the first few minutes after meeting." To the French, their home is their fortress, a shield from the outside world. Even if a Frenchman had been entertained abroad, Nourissier added, he would hesitate to return the invitation for fear that his lifestyle would be unworthy of his guests. He advised, "Foreigners who find us so little hospitable and who complain about how difficult it is to get to know French families should never forget that this shame is real, and in most cases justified." Based on French cooking skills and their one-on-one charm, we found that not being invited based on an unworthy lifestyle hard to believe.

There were, however, two phrases and two qualities that, because of their repetitions in daily life, could be isolated as French characteristics.

The first phrase: "It's not my fault," colloquially, *C'est pas ma faute.* The French either never admitted to doing anything wrong or blamed someone else for a misdeed. The second phrase: "It doesn't exist," *Ça n'existe pas,* was spoken if one did not know the answer, was either too busy or unwilling to cooperate, or if something was not available, like pasteurized milk at the Neuilly market.

The first quality was indifference.

When we arrived in Neuilly in March 1965, one of my first chores was to find the closest places to buy food for the family. I looked forward to shopping at the open-air market twice a week on the avenue de Neuilly where farmers from the country displayed their fresh produce, for which France is famous, and fresh-cut flowers that lasted almost two weeks. Three-month-old Debby slept in the Swiss carriage, which we had bought in Zurich, and eighteen-month-old Steven sat in a small extension chair in the front. The carriage was not geared for the extra weight, but I had no choice, even though I carried as many items as I could in my French expandable string bag. One morning, after the purchases were put on the rack below, as we neared the apartment, everything gave out. A corner of Steven's chair tipped into the carriage. I panicked that Debby would be hurt. I stood Steven next to me on the sidewalk in order to figure out how I could proceed safely. Passers-by just passed by. I finally carried Debby home, having placed Steven and the purchases in the carriage. A similar incident, but with a ripped shopping bag, once happened in New York. Three people began to gather and return the rolling apples and oranges. One of them gave me the plastic bag in which he was carrying a newly purchased book. These were spontaneous, friendly gestures. In Neuilly, no one came to the rescue.

Four years later, there was a second incident. I was pregnant. I had a toothache. My appointment with the dentist in Paris was early in the morning, and while hurrying to give the children their breakfast, I had no time for my own. When I returned by metro to Neuilly, I decided to go to the open market, which was on my way home. In my delicate condition and with no food, I felt faint. I grabbed onto one of the poles that the farmers used to support the canvasses covering the stalls and slowly slid to the ground. Again no one helped. Fortunately the moment passed. I was able to continue home admittedly walking close to buildings on the way in case the weakness recurred.

Jean-Benoit Nadeau, coauthor of *Sixty Million Frenchmen Can't Be Wrong*, offered what seemed to be the best explanation of this indifference. The French, unlike the Americans, do not think being liked is important. He added, "Being appreciated, being in power, being right. Yes. Being liked? No." To help a stranger might appear as an attempt to be friendly, or liked, or both. In both cases, I needed help. Being liked was a nonissue.

Politically, President de Gaulle also had complaints about his own people's indifference, calling it their "every man for himself" attitude. In his book *The Trouble with France*, Alain Peyrefitte, the education minister in the French government, expanded on de Gaulle's disappointments with his people. He claimed that they acted like children. They detested the state until there was a threat to their existence. Then they waited passively for the authorities to do everything for them, while refusing to make the necessary changes due to their mistrust of these authorities. De Gaulle asked, "How can France be governed if the French are ungovernable? I can't do anything for France without the French." The only solution to their independence, de Gaulle offered, was to "rally around their national pride." He warned that if they did not do this they would "dissolve in mediocrity."

The second quality was love of talking.

The challenge was to score as many points in a conversation as possible in as long a time as it took. The only prerequisite was to find a compelling subject and pepper it with a dash of Gallic wit and perhaps a hint of irony. Talking endlessly indicates knowledge to the French, and, above all, they respect an intellectual.

At a dinner party to which we were invited, the hostess, originally from Holland married to an American diplomat, was confronted by one of her French guests about the escalation of U.S. forces in Vietnam. He claimed that the Americans were trying to take it over as a sphere of influence now that the French were gone. And why did President Eisenhower refuse to send air coverage to French troops when the tide was turning against them at Dien Bien Phu? According to statistics, by 1954 the U.S. had spent $2.5 billion to finance the French in Indochina, or 80 percent of French expenditures for the war. This was more than France received in Marshall Plan aid from America to rebuild her shattered postwar economy.

The rebuttal of my hostess was immediate and pro-American as only a naturalized American can be. She reminded her guest that the French were fighting merely to maintain their presence in Indochina for economic reasons, while America's more noble cause was halting the spread of communism in Southeast Asia. France could have taken her case to the United Nations at that time but probably feared that the issue of French colonialism in North Africa also would come up for discussion. Other Americans at the table did not enter the conversation, thinking it would be rude, although joining in is welcomed by the French as a way to continue the momentum. As my hostess said to me later, "Why should I be polite? He wasn't." It took a born Netherlander to come to the aid of her party.

62

At one of my own dinners for Philippe's office colleagues, one of the men began to talk about the economic challenge of American firms in Paris. The soup was served, and he talked. The main course – he was still talking. Dessert followed – an end was in sight. The men adjourned to another room. The women remained seated. Speaking about our children might not have been intellectual, but it was a relief.

Voltaire, the great eighteenth-century writer, addressed the nature of unlimited talk: "The necessity of saying something, the perplexity of having nothing to say, and a desire of being witty, are the three circumstances which alone are capable of making even the greatest writer ridiculous." In a social setting, we were sometimes obliged to live through this "necessity."

If the source of French behavior could be found, the education of children seemed to be the logical starting place. We observed this firsthand when Steven entered the *jardin d'enfants,* a cross between nursery school and kindergarten, in September 1966, a month before his third birthday. The Cours Montaigne was a pleasant, private school in a converted private house on the rue Charles Lafitte. The children were mainly French. Others were from international families in which the fathers worked for subsidiaries of commercial or legal firms. A few were in diplomatic service. This group, mostly English-speaking, became the base of our friendships in France. As in most countries, such friendships begin where the children are.

We marveled at the girls in their neat dresses and the boys wearing short pants even in the coldest weather. Leather shoes were part of their daily attire. Sneakers and blue jeans were nowhere to be seen. Only Steven wore long pants and saddle shoes, easily spotted as the little American boy.

French parents were seen as authoritarian, as were French teachers. Children were to be corrected, not pampered. They were taught respect from their earliest years, such as shaking hands with adults and answering questions directly, be it to Mademoiselle, Madame, or Monsieur.

These observations are from Steven's three years of French schooling, from the *jardin d'enfants,* through two primary grades, numbered in descending order: the *douzième*, or twelfth, equal to the first grade, and the *onzième*, the eleventh, equal to the second grade. Debby also attended the *jardin d'enfants* in 1968 when she was three, a year prior to our return to America. The manner of teaching was different from the American way, but no one I knew objected to the final results.

The method was by rote, whether it was writing the alphabet or the teacher's *dictée* (dictation) in the child's notebook. In art, a given subject was copied on the same line. However, time was set aside to draw a *dessin libre* (a picture of one's choice). Homework was assigned daily.

We once entered Steven's room to wake him up for school only to find him already dressed, sitting at his table working on his arithmetic homework. He clearly knew what was expected of him at school.

Writing: Teacher wrote the first line. Steven, age four and a half, then copied the words beneath.

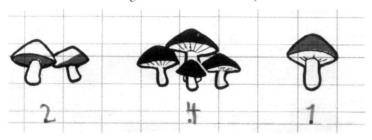

Arithmetic: Learning numbers related to objects.

Art: copying the first drawing.

Children must learn to conform. There were no allowances for individual differences. Initiative and open discussion were discouraged. All instruction was alike and accepted without question. One must pay attention – no talking in class. There were good marks for achievement but ridicule from teachers and other children for improper behavior. Even during recess, which, at the Cours Montaigne, might include a walk to the Bois de Boulogne three blocks away in good weather (right), play time was usually done in an orderly manner.

Spring 1967

64

When I came for Steven one morning after school, I noticed that the children all had been given workbooks with a picture on each page of one letter of the alphabet with objects or animals corresponding to it. Steven had no workbook. I asked the teacher why, and her answer was in keeping with the criterion for the age group: "He cannot even draw a house yet." She gratuitously added, "He has no sense of group discipline. He wants to touch and see everything and has very little patience to wait until things are given to the children by the teacher. He is not aggressive with other children, just with things." Steven was being taught in a foreign language. He was the youngest in a class of twenty-nine children, ages three and four. Even though there was an assistant in the classroom, it was beyond the eight to ten children per teacher that the American pediatric guru Dr. Benjamin Spock considered ideal for that age group. When I discussed with our French pediatrician, Dr. Mande, whether I should take Steven out of school, he was adamant. "That would be a defeat and confusing to the child. The teacher is trained for this work. Let her cope."

I then went to a bookstore to buy a children's alphabet book with pictures, which I cut and pasted into an attractive loose-leaf folder, so he could have one of his own. It was beyond my understanding why a three-year-old child should feel left out. The next day, he reported, "Everyone wants one like mine." Months later, when Steven did draw a house, I had the picture baked into a small porcelain dish in a specialty shop in Paris as a souvenir of the *jardin d'enfants*.

Steven's first report card in December read, "Although an intelligent and alert child for his age, Steven is still very unstable and undisciplined." When I asked Philippe, my European-educated husband, what "unstable" meant, he said that to the French it meant that Steven had no patience to sit for an hour stringing beads. "Undisciplined" meant that he was a normal, American three-year-old. As Dr. Mande suggested, they would just have to cope.

Another morning, another incident. An American mother coming from school was obviously in a foul mood. I could not imagine what the problem was until she offered, "If they ever tape my daughter's mouth again for talking, they'll hear from me." Sweet, happy, little Mary did not realize that chatting with the girl next to her was forbidden.

I once asked Steven's teacher if the book from which the students were learning to read, published decades ago, would ever be updated. Her reply was almost indignant. "Why should it be? It teaches them to read." American educational book companies, geared for selling frequent, new publications to schools, would be reduced to tears or imminent bankruptcy. My only real complaint was that the common cold was considered minor enough to keep children in school, infecting the whole class until everyone was coughing and sneezing. In America, a sick child would be sent home immediately.

The role of parents was to bring children to and from school – no PTA, no bake sale to raise money for extra equipment, no Strawberry Festival. The only event we were invited to was the end-of-year Prize Awarding ceremony, where each student's marks were read aloud and various honors were given to the highest academic achievers. In the middle of the ceremony, and before we knew what he was up to, uninhibited Steven walked to the front where the headmaster, Monsieur de Just, was sitting and reading the marks, climbed on his lap, and looked at his notes as if he could be of some assistance. The parents laughed out loud. The headmaster had no other choice but to smile and accept the incident in good humor while motioning to Steven's teacher to put him back in his seat immediately. Steven remained unmolded in the French image.

In his sociological study of life in southeastern France, *Village in the Vaucluse*, Laurence Wylie explained the effects of such educational methods on the French mind. Whether they applied to the Cours Montaigne with its rather sophisticated mix of students in this Paris suburb is uncertain, but it was interesting to read what we ourselves were experiencing.

Wylie concluded that since spontaneity is not officially recognized in the educational system, children learn that their personalities must be kept constantly under control. Given the shame they must endure for not conforming, he asked, "How can a child avoid feeling as he grows up that people are ready to assail him collectively with the force of public scorn whenever he deviates from the behavior that is expected of him?" Confronted with an unresponsive, centralized French government, the individual later feels manipulated rather than being able to participate in a welcoming political process. In turn, he "manipulates the system to accomplish what may be legally unattainable." The Paris-based, American CBS bureau chief, David Schoenbrun, did not think that the "constant competition, harping on distinction or disgrace" of the school system made children better human beings. He blamed the rivalry, jealousy, and discord of competitive schools for the constant crisis of French politics.

As we learned, the respect that the French hold for their intellectuals was mainly reserved for graduates of *les grandes écoles,* the elite schools that provide the talented leaders who run the country. The most prestigious were: the *École Normale Supérieure,* geared for teaching and politics, the school of Georges Pompidou, who succeeded Charles de Gaulle as president in 1969; the *École Polytechnique* for engineering, sciences, and originally for the military; the *École Nationale d'Administration,* the ENA, which focuses on civil service, administration, and business management, founded in 1945 by de Gaulle. High government positions were filled from its ranks. To be among the elite was the aim of the most motivated students (and their parents), in the French educational system.

66

On the lighter side, the French sense of humor and capacity for fun were evident to me even ten years before at a *Reveillon* in Paris, the Christmas eve gaiety, when, if you did not strike up a conversation with those at the next table, or indeed with the whole nightclub, you were not in the spirit of the evening. In the sixties, my appreciation of French humor was reinforced in the satirical weekly, *Le Canard Enchâiné,* that not only lampooned self-important politicians and dignitaries, but paid irreverent attention to the latest mini-skirt craze or to the heated controversy over the birth control pill.

Paris was still the fashion leader in the sixties. American buyers flooded in by invitation to see the latest collections of the well-known couture houses. The knee, almost to the thigh, was in. Although Mary Quant in London was credited with the youthful fashion, it was adapted by such famous French designers as Pierre Cardin and Courrèges, who applied their unique touches to the mini for the benefit of their fashion-conscious clientele. Copies surfaced in Saks Fifth Avenue and Alexander's in New York where high fashion was made affordable. When my mother visited in the summer of 1969 to await the birth of my third child, I reserved seats at the House of Dior knowing that she would enjoy a fashion show, one of the great, free, daily happenings in Paris.

La Messe de Mini. The Mini-Mass
Moisan. *Le Canard Enchâiné,* December 21, 1966

A diligent priest oversees his faithful, female parishioners at mass, as they kneel on their prie-Dieu. French women of all shapes and sizes would not be denied the latest mini-skirt fashion, even if their garters showed.

67

As for the pill, on July 25, 1968, the Vatican issued the encyclical letter of Pope Paul VI, *Humanae Vitae – On the Regulation of Birth*. At my annual exam a year before, I had asked my doctor about the status of the pill in this predominantly Catholic country. His reply: "We're working on it." Opponents of the pill claimed that family planning came from America, like racketeers and kidnapping.

The encyclical addressed the value of conjugal love and the obligation of married couples to procreate as a divine duty. Any artificial means intended to prevent procreation, such as the pill, were "absolutely excluded." Contraception was only permitted for health reasons. Bishops were instructed to guide priests in defining the church's teachings on marriage, and to doctors to counsel married couples in the proper doctrinal direction.

The obligations of married couples were clear, but for the unmarried, we were assured by Françoise, our savvy helper (*bonne à tout faire*), age nineteen, that priests were understanding in the ways of the world. The *Canard Enchâiné* picked up on the subtleties of priestly duties within two consecutive weeks.

— On ne fait pas des enfants de chœur avec la pilule.

Effel. *Canard Enchâiné,* Aug. 7, 1968

According to the encyclical:
Priest to the Bishop:
"One does not make a children's choir with the pill."

— Mon Père, j'ai pris la pilule.
— Combien de fois, mon enfant ?

Moisan. *Canard Enchâiné,* Aug. 14, 1968

According to human nature:
Confessor: "Father, I took the pill."
Priest: "How many times, my child?"

68

The French lived for their generous summer holidays. The *congés payés,* or workers' paid vacations, began in 1936 as a policy of the Socialist premier, Léon Blum. It since had become an absolute right based on time accumulated annually, not to be tampered with. In 1966, Janet Flanner reported in her *Paris Journal* that two million Frenchmen vacationed in July and another two million in August. President de Gaulle urged his countrymen to stagger their time off within the two summer months in order to diffuse the traffic jams and overcrowded resorts expected during their weeks of fun, hopefully in the sun.

«*Les Vacances du Moi d'Aout*» August Vacation
J. Lap. *Le Canard Enchâiné,* July 27, 1966.

President de Gaulle, imagined here relaxing on a beach, also was entitled to a vacation. The Elysée was closed, his ministers and advisers were away. His current political worry list – the USSR, Abyssinia, Cambodia, Polynesia – was put aside while he focused on the obligatory sun tan. The world was suspended while the French chose from among their favorite pastimes – hiking, fishing, sightseeing, or taking photos for the family album.

As Americans living in France, we loved Paris in the summer when the French had gone south to the Côte d'Azur beaches or to their country homes within a sixty-mile radius of the capital. Although vital services and most restaurants were closed (as the French described it, "There isn't a cat in Paris"), the local vacuum was filled by foreign tourists. An estimated million and a half Americans went abroad in 1966, even though President Johnson had appealed to them to stay home and spend their dollars in the U.S. But they were determined to see the world before the cost of the Vietnam War or de Gaulle's policy of buying up gold, an attack on the basic monetary standard, affected the favorable five-francs-to-the-dollar exchange rate.

Regardless of the generous French summer vacations, we limited ours to school breaks during the year, in order to accumulate time for a trip to the States. A five-day maximum, including going and returning, were suited to the endurance of two children under five-years of age, if not of their parents, aware of the demands of travel, meals, rest stops, and hotels. We did not make reservations, believing that off-season travel would allow flexibility of choice in picturesque locations. We forgot that all schools were on vacation.

On one motor trip to Honfleur, the charming fishing port in Normandy, the children had their first experience at restaurant dining. The food, to which they were not accustomed, was left untouched at a restaurant alongside the pier of the Old Basin, moving us to buy baguettes, cheese, yogurt, milk, and fruit for the remaining days. Steven was delighted with the cruise barges moored at the pier and proceeded to pull on the tethered rope of one of them. To our surprise, the barge began to move a few feet. The owner, dining at the same restaurant, waved us away. We obliged immediately.

Driving on a dirt road in the rich farmland of Normandy, we came across mottled brown cows behind a fence. The children insisted on feeding them with straw lying on the ground. Steven declared that he wanted to be a farmer when he grew up. Debby preferred to be a ballerina.

Since distances in Europe between countries are shorter than between states in America, our next trip was to a chalet in Verbier in the eastern Swiss Alps at the invitation of Philippe's sister during a Christmas vacation. The bright sun shone on the snow-covered slopes where the sledding, or luging, was perfect. The joy of activity and red cheeks of the children playing outdoors all day were worth the trip. Not so at bedtime, when the altitude and unfamiliar surroundings played havoc with their sleep. I was up numerous times during the night, with bare feet on cold floors, reassuring them that if they would get to sleep they would have another fun day of luging.

The food shops in the village with their cheeses, fondue sets, and smoked meats were fond reminders of Zurich. At a nearby clothing shop, I purchased a pair of woolen slippers to make the nights bearable. Returning to our warm apartment in Neuilly was my fun part.

Exploring foreign places was an enjoyable part of living abroad, but news of the world kept crowding in.

[V]
AMERICA
VIETNAM WAR, CIVIL RIGHTS

VIETNAM : 20 ANS DE SALE GUERRE

Le Président Directeur Général de la Viet War and Cⁱᵉ.

Moisan. *Le Canard Enchâiné*, June 15, 1966

By mid-March 1965, when I arrived with the children in Paris, U.S. bombing campaigns on North Vietnamese targets, Operation Rolling Thunder, had begun. French newspapers and magazines carried photographs of a defoliated Vietnam with refugees living in camps and bodies burned by napalm. On March 8, the first American military units had landed in South Vietnam. By the end of the year, American troop strength was nearly two hundred thousand. During the early sixties, President Kennedy had escalated the amount of advisers sent to Vietnam based on executive powers without the authorization of Congress or public knowledge. As casualties mounted, so did public dissent.

In an Asian extension of the cold war, the Soviet Union allied with Communist China and its growing power in the region. Fear of Red Chinese influence spurred U.S. commitment to SEATO, the Southeast Asia Treaty Organization, signed in 1954 to protect its members, of which South Vietnam was one, from armed aggression. Lost opportunities abounded. We read that at the Versailles Peace Conference in 1919 after World War I, Ho Chi Minh tried to appeal for Vietnamese independence but was turned away without being heard. When Ho asked President Truman in 1945 for economic aid eight times in five months, his appeals went unanswered on the grounds that Washington did not recognize his Democratic Republic of Vietnam. In 1950 China and the Soviet Union did. Both became North Vietnam's prime military suppliers. Communism to Ho was the means to achieve his life's goal of national independence.

Charles de Gaulle warned the U.S. that being staunchly against communism would reinforce the impression that Communists were the champions of Third World national independence. He also urged the unification of North and South Vietnam and the withdrawal of all foreign forces. To the military planners in Washington, this meant the rapid fall of Vietnam to communism and probably of Laos and Cambodia as well. In his detailed book, *The Vantage Point,* President Johnson reacted, "I made it a rule for myself and for the U.S. government simply to ignore President de Gaulle's attacks on our policies and the doubts he had raised about the value of our pledges." Johnson relied on the historic friendship between the French and American people.

OPPOSITE PAGE: In a stark, French, anti-war cartoon, "Vietnam: Twenty Years of Dirty War," the years range from 1946, when France renewed its colonial rule, to 1966, when Lyndon Johnson, the "President Director General of the Viet and C' (Communist) War," committed U.S. forces to full-scale war. Johnson wears a helmet and a uniform covered with medals shaped like crosses that extend to a war cemetery. Behind him, the Statue of Liberty wears a gas mask and holds a napalm torch whose smoke wafts toward explosions of cluster bombs dropped on Vietnam from B-52s. Bodies float down the Mekong River (left) while soldiers and a tank (right) approach the devastation. The bank buildings behind the statue and the financial chart on Johnson's eight-star helmet might reflect French suspicions that the war was being waged for America's profit.

During our four years in France, we watched as American-backed South Vietnamese leaders often engaged in infighting or ineffectively countering Vietcong attacks. In his series, "The Strategy of Error," which began in the *International Herald Tribune* on February 28, 1968, C. L. Sulzberger wrote that the problem for our troops was how to defeat unfamiliar jungle warfare and quick-strike ambushes. He also noted that there was danger in imposing democracy on those who had neither the tradition nor willingness to accept it.

Ho Chi Minh, backed by the military in Hanoi, the North Vietnamese capital, ignored forty-five U.S. peace feelers from 1965 to 1967, frustrating our intentions to gradually disengage from the war. In February 1967, he replied to President Johnson's letter suggesting direct talks: "The Vietnamese people have never done any harm to the United States, but contrary to the commitments made by its representative at the Geneva conference of 1954, the United States government has constantly intervened in Vietnam for the purpose of prolonging the division of Vietnam and of transforming South Vietnam into an American colony and military base." Actually, although supporting the agreements made by the other Geneva participants, the U.S. and South Vietnam did not sign the final declaration in case of renewed aggression.

Hanoi's conditions to begin peace talks were for the U.S. to stop unconditionally both the bombing of the country and, as Ho described, its use of "barbaric methods of warfare such as napalm, chemicals, and toxic gases to massacre our compatriots, destroy their crops, and level their villages." It was not lost on him that activists from various universities in America staged protests when recruiters arrived on campus from Dow Chemical, the manufacturer of napalm for use in Vietnam. In his letter, Ho added that support for his cause came from "all the people of the world, including large segments of the American people."

As Americans abroad, we were incensed when Vice President Hubert Humphrey visited Paris on April 7, 1967, on the fiftieth anniversary of America's entry into World War I, to attend a ceremony at the statue of George Washington on the place d'Iéna and to lay a wreath at the Tomb of the Unknown Soldier at the Arc de Triomphe. Communist students were out in full force carrying on antiwar protests. The newspapers reported that they tore down and burned the American flag from the American Cathedral, broke windows of American Express offices, hung a "U.S. Go Home" banner from the Eiffel Tower, and pelted two Marine guards and a black man in an American Legion uniform with eggs and red paint. The American embassy protested that the police stood by and did nothing to protect the Americans. The police later apologized. Before a luncheon that de Gaulle gave for Humphrey, the two of them had a private forty-minute meeting. We assumed that the subject of Vietnam was discussed based on Humphrey's curt statement to the press: "No comment right now, whatsoever."

What we knew firsthand about the Vietnam War, besides de Gaulle's convictions, the media coverage, and our own frustrations, came from two American sources. The first was Joe Thorndike, the executive editor during my years at *Horizon Magazine*, while he was vacationing in Europe. His news: The unpopular Vietnam War was dividing the country, and the social reforms of the Great Society were floundering with the worsening reports from the war front, with race riots and antiwar protests at home. The second was an overheard conversation of two American officers on leave from Vietnam with whom I shared a taxi from the airport in Paris after returning one weekend from London. They spoke of "Nam" and the hideous conditions of jungle warfare. I wanted to say something but did not want to intrude on their privacy. I regretted not thanking them as an American for their sacrifices in this remote, confusing war.

I was feeling isolated and unpatriotic, not being able to share in the sentiments and debates swirling around the political issues. Reading about events a continent away was no substitute for being among one's own while they were happening. It was time to touch home base. The opportunity came when we were told of a summer rental on Long Beach Island at the New Jersey shore beginning July 1, 1967. We were to spend two weeks at the beach and two in Elizabeth with my parents. Pediatric checkups for the children also were on the agenda. To Debby, the sandy Jersey coastline was the Neuilly sandbox in the square, a tall television aerial behind the next house was the Eiffel Tower, and the annoying sand flies were *"les petites mouches."*

When we got to Elizabeth in mid-July, we were to experience events up close. A four-day riot among the black population in neighboring Newark broke out, with a total of twenty-five dead and more than a thousand injured. Major stores were closed, and a curfew paralyzed half the city. All car traffic stopped between 10 P.M. and dawn. The atmosphere in Elizabeth was tense. We did not go far from the apartment we were sharing with my parents, fearing that there would be a spillover from Newark. We only had telephone visits with friends.

An uncle who drove us to the airport asked jokingly, "So, do you think violence is as 'American as cherry pie'?", quoting a statement of H. Rap Brown at his news conference in Washington, D.C., on July 27. Since May, Brown had been the black national chairman of the Student Nonviolent Coordinating Committee (SNCC), following the leadership of the radical Stokely Carmichael. What began as a nonviolent movement to register black voters in the South had turned militant in an effort to energize progress. Militancy was outpacing Dr. Martin Luther King Jr.'s nonviolent approach to civil rights. In August 1965, a six-day riot in the Watts section of Los Angeles was fueled by black unemployment, poor housing facilities in ghetto-like conditions, and inadequate education.

Dr. King blamed Congress for creating the atmosphere for the riots by not addressing the high rate of black unemployment and having little concern for slum conditions, which endangered the lives of children. But he saw no turning back from the success of nonviolence in the advancement of civil rights, for which he had won the Nobel Peace Prize in 1964.

College students and others of draft age faced the reality of the Vietnam War and the interruption of their lives. One of their slogans: "You can't trust anyone over thirty." Anti-war activists included the Berrigan brothers, Philip, a Catholic priest serving as associate pastor in a black Baltimore parish, and Daniel, a Jesuit priest and poet. With a few supporters, they defaced or set fire to Maryland's Selective Service draft records both in Baltimore and Catonsville, symbols to them of America's misplaced power and exploitation of its youth. For these and other acts of civil disobedience, they both served prison terms, but as Daniel wrote, "The time is past when good men can remain silent."

Hippies proliferated. Many saw them as self-absorbed, indulged flower children with their unkempt hair, tie-dye shirts, beads, and sandals. Ex-president Harry Truman thought they were not "spanked enough as they grew up." Growing drug use was the vilest of evils. Those who were part of this counterculture dropped out of society in what one sociologist claimed was a refusal to accept the norms and patterns of adult behavior. American cartoons, below, show Herblock's Nero-like Congress fiddling while cities burned (left) and Bill Maudlin's camouflaged soldiers in Vietnam (right) joking about hippies.

'I'm a Flower Child.'

1967 Herblock cartoon. © by the Herb Block Foundation. Courtesy of Library of Congress.

© 1967 by Bill Mauldin Courtesy of the Mauldin Estate.

After our vacation, our return to the calm boulevard Jean Mermoz and life in a country where the cream of her youth was not being decimated made us grateful that Steven and Debby would avoid the worst of the sixties. Even the required discipline of the French school system seemed comforting. Obeying rules and respecting the authority of teachers and parents at a young age were valuable things. When Steven went for his checkup in New Jersey with Dr. Schotland, he shook hands with him in the French manner. The good doctor was impressed but was quick to note, "He'll lose that soon enough." We knew he was right. But we enjoyed it while we could.

I sat in the square watching my two children in the sandbox with their pails and shovels "digging a tunnel to America," as they said. For the first time, I was quite content to live abroad. France had its virtues. As Steven approached his fourth birthday, he was still a bundle of energy, irrepressible in the ways of a four-year-old. I wrote home, "It looks like another banner year for his kindergarten teacher."

The war worsened, the riots continued. The My Lai massacre in March 1968, when a U.S. Army infantry company shot up a South Vietnamese village, killing a few hundred unarmed civilians, including women, children, and babies, was proof of what the war was doing to our soldiers. Deteriorating morale, extensive use of marijuana, and insubordination to superior officers were some of the reports reaching us back home.

But a change was in the air. On April 1, 1968, I heard a rebroadcast of the announcement President Johnson made the night before from the Oval Office in the White House. He confirmed both a partial ending of bombing in North Vietnam and that he would not run for another term in November. It was as much of a shock to us in France as it was in America to those who thought Johnson was a man hungry for power, a political arm-twister for whom the presidency was the ultimate prize. But Johnson, the tall Texan whom his detractors called a cowboy, admitted, "Power can lose its charm when a man has known it as many years as I had." The chant of the crowds, "Hey hey, LBJ, how many kids did you kill today?" weighed heavily on him. After his announcement, he wrote, "All that I could do I had done." De Gaulle believed Johnson's decision was courageous, a move in the right direction.

To President Johnson's credit, his Great Society made important progress in the social issues plaguing the country. The Civil Rights Act that he signed on July 2, 1964, was called "the most far-reaching civil rights law since Reconstruction days." Among its aims was an end to discrimination in employment, public accommodations, and federally aided programs. In August 1965, as we were adjusting to our first year in France, Johnson signed the Voting Rights Act that guaranteed Blacks the long-overdue right denied to them through White racist threats and discriminatory poll taxes in the South. Poll watchers then could be assigned to monitor elections if any duly registered person complained of being denied the right to vote.

Johnson knew that the civil rights legislation that he shepherded and that began with the initiative of John Kennedy signaled the death of the Democratic party in the South. But the time to address racial injustice, as elsewhere, had come. Johnson was determined to do the right thing.

In the fall of 1968, we again applied for an absentee ballot. It would be our last vote away from America. Democrat Hubert Humphrey ran against Republican Richard Nixon but did not disassociate himself early enough from the failed Vietnam policies of Lyndon Johnson and from ineffective law and order in the racial disturbances of the cities. The people wanted a change. Richard Nixon claimed he had a plan to end the war. He won.

Shortly after his inauguration in 1969, Nixon sanctioned the bombing of Vietcong sanctuaries in Cambodia, claiming that he would negotiate with the North Vietnamese but only if they showed good faith. He would not be "the first president of the United States to lose a war," echoing the previous determination of Lyndon Johnson.

Nixon later was to describe the Vietnam War as one of "mutual miscalculation." He was the fifth American leader to miscalculate, from Harry Truman's backing of the French in their efforts to reclaim their Indochinese colony when Japanese occupation ended after World War II; to escalations by Presidents Eisenhower and Kennedy in the form of direct aid and advisers to Premier Diem in South Vietnam; to Lyndon Johnson's use of the Tonkin Gulf incident in August 1964 to secure congressional legitimacy for U.S. actions against North Vietnam. The sequence of events in the Tonkin Gulf was never fully verified, or, as some claim, manipulated by the administration to secure official backing to pursue the war.

On January 23, 1973, Nixon announced that a cease-fire agreement to end the Vietnam War had been initialed in Paris. It was the "peace with honor" he had sought, as he paid tribute to those Americans who served in Vietnam and to those who had lost their lives. He especially thanked President Lyndon Johnson, vilified in his lifetime, but who cared deeply about achieving a lasting peace. Johnson died the day before the announcement was made.

The "Vietnam syndrome," referring to the public's resistance to involvement in a war of choice abroad that is believed to be immoral, would haunt America well into the future. President Eisenhower once explained his decision not to intervene directly in Indochina at the time of France's last stand at Dien Bien Phu in 1954. Such involvement, he claimed, would lead to charges of imperialistic ambitions: "Without allies and associates, the leader is just an adventurer like Genghis Khan." It seemed a comment worth remembering.

[VIa]
1967: THE SIX-DAY WAR

THE UNITED NATIONS PODIUM

"The Conception of Individual Nations Has Lost All Significance." Charles de Gaulle, April 1948

Moisan. *Le Canard Enchâiné,* June 21, 1967

Members of the United Nations, depicted as a multilingual Tower of Babel within a semicircle of their national flags, reflect both their alliances either with Israel or the Arab states and the outcome of the Six-Day War of June 1967 in the Middle East. Israel (Moshe Dayan), the winner, is on top, hoisted by its ally, the United States (Lyndon Johnson), and restrained by its antagonist, Soviet Russia (Premier Kosygin, with shoe flying). Egypt (Gamal Abdel Nasser, clutching Johnson), had closed the Strait of Tiran to Israeli shipping, thereby opposing England (a pipe-smoking Harold Wilson), in agreement with America that the Strait was an international waterway. Statesmen from Spain, Soviet Russia, and Africa form the lower half of the tower. France, at the center of the base (Charles de Gaulle, holding the glasses of Israel's prime minister, Levi Eshkol, whose foot is on de Gaulle's head), had warned Israel not to fire the first shot. UN Secretary General U Thant (below left) seems ill, possibly for provoking the war by unilaterally withdrawing UNEF, the UN Emergency Force, from the Sinai. Pope Paul VI sits in the referee's chair (far left) while a dove of peace above him flies from the H-bomb held menacingly by China (Mao Tse-tung, on his high perch). Two observers (below right) comment, "It is the Tower of Babel. They swear in every language."

On June 5, 1967, a month before we left on our American holiday, the Six-Day War broke out. Egypt, Jordan, Syria, Iraq, Algeria, Sudan, and Kuwait all declared war on Israel. Saudi Arabia, Morocco, Yemen, and Tunisia also pledged their support. As the cold war had spread to Southeast Asia, with America and Russia backing different sides in the Vietnam War, the two superpowers now were to confront each other in the Middle East. In cold war mode, Soviet warships and the American Sixth Fleet were poised in the eastern Mediterranean to protect their interests: the Soviets pro-Egypt, the U.S. pro-Israel.

A call went out to the Jewish community in Paris to attend an emergency meeting at the home of a young French lawyer, living near the Luxembourg Gardens, who had taken the initiative to discuss the threat to Israel. The vulnerability of Israel's cities to air attack was the main concern. From el-Arish in Sinai to Tel Aviv it was seven minutes by air, and less over the twelve miles from Jordan to Tel Aviv at Israel's narrowest point. About thirty people had gathered to see what they could do to help. Several Holocaust survivors from the Hitler years and a few Israelis were among those present.

The lawyer began by mentioning members of the prominent Rothschild banking family in France as the rallying point of moral and financial support when there was a specific need in the French-Jewish community. He felt that this took initiative away to meet a crisis or raise funds on its own. It was time to begin thinking independently. The group then was asked for volunteers to board Israeli children until the danger in the Middle East was past. Everyone agreed. Homes that did not have the space somehow would make space. A week later, we were informed that the Israelis would not part with their children. They felt that whatever happened, at least they would be together.

The meeting began with a review of the conflict.

On May 22, 1967, Egypt's president, Gamal Abdel Nasser, ordered the Gulf of Aqaba and the Strait of Tiran closed to Israeli shipping. Ten years earlier during the Eisenhower administration, this passageway leading south to the Red Sea had been designated an international waterway, with no nation having the right to prevent its free access. President Nasser disagreed, claiming that the Gulf and the Strait were Egyptian territory. Israeli ships or others headed for Israel would not pass. President Johnson called Nasser's claim to control the waterway illegal, an act of war, justifying Israel's right to self-defense. From Elath, Israel's port parallel to Aqaba in Jordan, the Gulf was Israel's commercial outlet to Africa and Asia through which came vital oil supplies from the shah's government in Iran. Abba Eban, Israel's foreign minister, called the blockade "an attempt to strangle a nation."

In addition to the closing of the waterway, two other incidents precipitated the war. On May 15, 1967, messages from the Kremlin falsely informed Syria and Egypt that Israel was massing its troops for an attack on Syria. In order to aid its Syrian ally, Nasser moved sixty thousand troops into the Sinai. On May 18, he demanded the removal of UNEF, the United Nations Emergency Force. It had been formed in March 1957 after England and France, with Israel's participation, failed in their attempt in October 1956 to regain access to the Suez Canal that Nasser had nationalized three months before. The United Nations demanded a cease-fire; the Anglo-French forces withdrew almost immediately. Israel withdrew only after UNEF was in place in the Sinai in 1957 and the Tiran Strait that lead to the blockaded Gulf of Aqaba was reopened.

UNEF's charge as peacekeeper was not only to oversee the withdrawal of Anglo-French and Israeli troops on Egyptian territory, but also to monitor the border between Egypt and Israel, the Gaza Strip, and the port of Sharm al-Sheikh that overlooked the Tiran Strait. Without consulting the General Assembly as to whether its mission had been completed successfully, U Thant, the secretary general of the United Nations, agreed to Egypt's demand to end UNEF's presence, based on Egypt's sovereign rights. Sharm al-Sheikh was left unguarded. De Gaulle could have influenced Nasser not to close the waterway, but what we saw instead was a change of attitude toward the Israel he once called "our friend, our ally." De Gaulle warned Abba Eban, "Do not make war. Do not be the first to shoot." The one who fired first would lose his support. In his autobiography, Eban recalled de Gaulle's reply when he reminded him that Israel only withdrew from Egypt in 1957 based on France's commitment to keep the Aqaba Gulf open. The French president answered that things had changed, "1967 was not 1957."

Regardless of de Gaulle, the French had been friendly to Israel in contrast to their hostility toward Algeria during its eight-year war for independence, with materiel provided by Egypt. Memories of bitter fighting and French losses within Algeria were not forgotten as two hundred thousand Muslims flooded into Paris after independence in 1962 looking for work among five million Parisians. The results were unemployment and an upsurge in crime. Any downturn in the labor market would be a disaster for Algerians and the five million relatives they were supporting back home.

The French military was particularly supportive of Israel, to the degree that de Gaulle accused it of being under Israeli influence. French pilots trained their Israeli counterparts in the effective use of France's superior aircraft, the Mirages, Mystères, Ouragans, and Vatour light bombers, which was the key to Israel's defense. With the threat of a Middle East war in 1967, de Gaulle embargoed fifty Mirages planes that already had been paid for. When the war erupted, a full arms embargo was imposed.

We then wanted to know what had caused de Gaulle to shift alliances.

Our lawyer-host repeated a French maxim, "France has neither friends nor enemies but only interests." De Gaulle saw that any aggravation of international tension would allow Soviets to take over the Arab world from which France had previously been excluded. Now that France no longer was embroiled with colonial problems, de Gaulle wanted to strengthen his traditional ties with the Arabs. Access to oil sources was still a priority. After the war, Raymond Aron, an astute French intellectual, professor, and philosopher wrote in his book *De Gaulle, Israel and the Jews* that a political turnabout can be forgiven and sometimes even admired, "but not when the objective smells of petrol and dictated by bad temper or wounded pride." The latter reference was to de Gaulle's complaint, "Israel did not follow my advice." In his final book, *Memoirs of Hope,* covering 1958-62, de Gaulle confirmed, "The Algerian crisis and the Suez affair had shut us out of the Arab world. I naturally intended to reestablish our position in this region where there had always been an active French presence, especially since the great political and strategic importance of the basins of the Nile, the Euphrates and the Tigris, of the Red Sea and the Persian Gulf, was now matched by economic power based on oil."

Finally, at the meeting, we discussed why Israel fired the first shot, having been warned not to do so, not only from France but also from America and Soviet Russia. We all gave our input based on which country we were from.

From an American point-of-view, we offered that although Lyndon Johnson was supportive of Israel's position, he was preoccupied with the Vietnam War, with no wish to open another front in the Middle East. Our ambassador in Amman previously had advised that supporting Israel in the conflict would undermine American influence in North Africa and the Middle East.

One of the Israelis present then stated that the decision by Israel to attack was not taken lightly. After the closing of the Tiran Strait, Prime Minister Levi Eshkol urged the Israel Defense Force to have patience. Arab tanks and aircraft outnumbered those of Israel three to one. Even Soviet foreign minister, Andrei Gromyko, told the Israeli ambassador to Moscow to remain calm, "Do not let your emotions get the better of you." Moshe Dayan, the minister of defense, had returned to active army duty to lead the Southern Command. He spoke of the critical element of surprise so vital to a small country like Israel with six hundred and fifty miles of hostile borders. One of Israel's rules was when in doubt, strike. Brigadier General Ariel Sharon declared that the problem was not so much the closing of the waterway as it was a case of Israel's survival.

As we adjourned, we could do no more than hope for a quick end to a war so critical to the survival of this small country against overwhelming odds.

Al-Hayat, Lebanon, May 31, 1967

On a wave of prewar euphoria, the Arab states are imagined impaling Israel on their tank guns. Shown clockwise: the Egyptian-led United Arab Command, Syria, Lebanon, and Jordan.

When King Hussein of Jordan returned from Egypt committed to a mutual alliance against Israel, he was sure that nine Arab armies were ready to act together. He declared, "There is no difference between one Arab people and another, no difference between one Arab army and another." President Abdul Rahman Aref of Iraq, reflecting Arab sentiment, was eager to "wipe Israel off the map . . . and God willing, meet in Haifa and Tel Aviv."

It was a short war. Israel called it "U Thant's war," as his agreement with Egypt to remove UNEF from Sinai condemned Israel to the aggressor's role. Israel achieved a huge military victory in the six days (132 hours) between June 5 and June 10. But the consequences were great: The Egyptian army and air force were destroyed, Egypt lost the Sinai, and Gaza did not return to Egyptian control. As reported in *Le Figaro,* Gaza was where "undercover guerrillas are being trained in sabotage, mining the borders of the kibbutzim, ambushes on the roads, grenades." It was a prelude to the militant al-Fatah, led by Abou Amar, also known as Yasser Arafat. Syria lost the Golan Heights, a thousand feet above sea level, from where shells rained down on the Jewish settlements in the Huleh Valley below for almost two decades. Jordan lost East Jerusalem and the West Bank. Israel had increased its territory threefold, and its population by a million Arabs. President de Gaulle predicted an uneasy future for Israel, with "border incidents, acts of sabotage, and frantic agitation."

At a press conference at the Elysée Palace on November 27, 1967, there was a strong reaction when President de Gaulle referred to the Jews as "an elite people, sure of themselves, and domineering *(dominateur)*." The reference, de Gaulle claimed, was one his father, Henri, a teacher in the day school he attended, had told his children long ago, even though Henri had not succumbed to the anti-Semitism of the political Right and did not believe that Alfred Dreyfus, the Jewish captain accused of treason in 1894, was guilty. The chief rabbi of France, Jacob Kaplan, in a private discussion with de Gaulle after a reception at the Elysée on January 1, 1968, explained that such a description of Jews could only sanction discrimination at the highest level. De Gaulle explained to him, as he had in his reply to Prime Minister David Ben-Gurion's letter two days before, that his statement was not meant to offend, but only "to emphasize the character, thanks to which this strong people could survive and remain themselves for nineteen centuries under appalling conditions."

Some French newspapers disagreed. *Le Monde* wrote that de Gaulle's words had "the unpleasant smell of anti-Semitism." Raymond Aron saw potential harm as the president of France had made it legitimate for anti-Semites to make themselves heard again and "to use the same language as before the Final Solution." And what if Israel had not shot first? Aron asked. "What would de Gaulle have offered Israel other than a press conference?" It was only *Le Figaro,* by printing both Ben-Gurion's letter, de Gaulle's reply, and acknowledging the need to calm emotions by his meeting with Rabbi Kaplan, that hoped it could be a prelude to a better rapport between France and Israel.

When we flew to Israel from Paris in 1968 to see Jerusalem united, we saw some of the war's devastation, such as the roof of the Church of the Dormition that had been set on fire. We were told that when the artist Marc Chagall heard that his stained-glass windows in the Hadassah Hospital in Ein Kerem had been damaged, he replied, "So I'll make new windows." In the garden of the Church of Gallicantu, where the apostle Peter heard the cock crow three times, we spoke with the Dutch head prelate who told us of the dismal hours the priests spent huddled downstairs listening to the sounds of gunfire. He saw a twentieth-century Israeli world clashing with the sixteenth-century Arab way of life. He was not happy that the private church road was now heavily trafficked. But, he added, "steps are being taken." Teddy Kollek, the charismatic mayor of the newly united city, was eager to accommodate the needs of the Christian and Muslim holy sites.

France's policy shift in the Middle East paid off. Nasser called de Gaulle a hero, "the only Western head of state on whose friendship the Arabs can depend." The reward for friendlier Arab relations was access to critical oil supplies. In April 1968, oil concessions were obtained in Saudi Arabia, with its billion barrels of oil beneath the sands. France also made a deal in Iraq to explore for oil. In return, the country would be supplied with French Mirage jets.

— Mes tapis contre votre nappe : ça boume ?

"My carpets for your underground flow: a deal?"

Moisan. *Le Canard Enchâiné,* December 13, 1967

President de Gaulle on his flying Mirage carpet, representing Mirage aircraft, extends his hand to the Iraqi oil merchant after offering what he considers a fair exchange. The cigar-smoking merchant, his white cape covering his rich, native attire, and his assistant in suit and tie, carry briefcases, seemingly prepared to do business. Symbolic Mirages and modern oil rigs contrast with simple shepherd life in the sun-drenched Iraqi landscape.

Human loss on both sides was a tragic by-product of the Six-Day War. Unresolved issues remained. From the hundreds of thousands of Arab refugees in squalid camps yearning for repatriation would rise the core of militants preparing to strike at Israel from within. Statehood for Palestine was a political goal for the distant future. For Israel, the central issues were its right to exist in secure and recognized borders and to live in peace with its neighbors.

86

[VIb]
JEWS OF FRANCE
A HISTORY

After the Six Day War in 1967, by blaming French sympathy for Israel on a Jewish-controlled media, President de Gaulle equated the Jews of both countries as one and the same. This was not only a breach of France's official state policy of secularism – loyalty to country first – but of Napoleon's historic prohibition of being a "nation within a nation." Raymond Aron predicted that de Gaulle had "knowingly opened a new period in Jewish history. . . . Everything again becomes possible. Everything starts over in an era of ill-will and suspicion." He added, "Many French Jews wept. They had lost their hero."

Regardless of such foreboding, a French opinion poll showed 56 percent pro-Israel, 2 percent pro-Arab, with 42 percent uncommitted. A few days before the war, spontaneous demonstrations and parades throughout Paris were joined by thousands of French of all faiths. Banners read "Israel, our friend, our ally," quoting de Gaulle's own words. Israeli and French flags were flown, and the anthems of both countries were sung by the animated crowd. Two thousand people volunteered to go to Israel to replace Israelis who had been mobilized. Among those who signed an appeal in support of Israel were the Spanish artist Pablo Picasso and the writer-philosopher Jean-Paul Sartre.

But a change was in the air. France's growing Muslim population from North Africa and de Gaulle's need for the natural resources of the Arabs, their oil, and commercial markets were to undermine Jewish friendship. The Jewish community once again had to reevaluate its position. Emigration to Israel, never before considered by those who had come to France seeking safe haven from eastern European anti-Semitism and pogroms, now was an option. Chafing under discrimination, unemployment, and poor living conditions, the Muslims found their scapegoat in the French Jews after the Six-Day War due to the Israeli occupation of the West Bank and Gaza and the plight of Palestinian refugees. For the Jews of France, a menacing element was beginning.

On a sunny June afternoon after school, I sat with three-year-old Steven on a bench in the "garden of repose" in front of the Saint-Pierre church in Neuilly, reading the newest adventures of *Asterix the Gaul,* the droll comic book of ancient Gallic history under Roman domination. We had just come from the *librairie*, the bookshop on the avenue du Roule, to buy this special treat to celebrate Steven's good report as his school term came to an end. Steven asked, "Are Hebrews permitted to sit in a church garden?" I assured him that anyone could sit wherever he liked in France. Then came a bigger surprise. He suddenly announced, "I'm going to kill all the Jews." I wondered where this was coming from. Could it be from his playmates at the Cours Montaigne, as Steven once described them to me – Didier, who "was naughty but had a nice face," Stanislaus, who was *"sage"* (good), Michel, "my best

88

friend?" Surely not from Sandrine or Marina, those perfectly behaved little girls. This was the *jardin d'enfants* with three- and four-year-olds. But parents talk, and children listen. I thought of young Charles de Gaulle and his father.

It was time to tell Steven a story about religious freedom in America. I explained that in old Russia the tsar killed Jews during a terrible pogrom. It was why our grandparents came to America. Steven was upset. "I'm not Jewish," he said firmly. "I don't want to get killed." And from the mouth of a fearful child came the basic impetus for Jewish conversion to Catholicism, such as occurred during the Spanish Inquisition in the fifteenth century. The evolution of religious toleration in France had a long and convoluted history. It became my spare-time reading after the children were in bed for the night.

During the centuries of the Catholic hereditary kings, it was not only the Jews but also the Protestant minority who surely learned from Psalms not to put their "faith in princes." After Spain's expulsion decree of March 31, 1492, eyewitnesses claimed that two hundred thousand to three hundred thousand Jews fled the country. (From a pre-statistical age, the actual numbers are impossible to confirm.) By land, the refugees found temporary haven in Portugal and the kingdom of Navarre. By sea, they went to other Catholic cities in Europe outside of Spanish and Portuguese influence, to Protestant countries, to North African cities, and throughout the Ottoman Empire. In France, the Jews had been expelled as early as 1394 but were welcomed to settle in Bordeaux as New Christians by edicts of Louis XI, twenty years after England's rule ended in 1453. The city's commerce would be revitalized. Jewish origins were to be hidden.

With the rise of Protestantism in Europe, the French Huguenots also suffered for their faith during the Wars of Religion from 1562 to 1598. The massacre of St. Bartholomew's Day, which began on August 24, 1572, resulted in ten thousand Huguenots being killed within a six-week period. In 1598, Henry IV of Navarre issued the Edict of Nantes, giving the Huguenots full toleration. But in 1685 Louis XIV revoked the Edict. Their choice was either to convert or go into exile. The four hundred thousand who left, (some claim six hundred thousand) enriched other European countries; pre-Revolutionary War colonies in America; and New France in Canada, with their talents as artisans, merchants, bankers, farmers, soldiers, and sailors. The revoking of the Edict by Louis XIV later was questioned by Voltaire in his story *Ingenuous*. The "man in black," a Protestant minister, asks: "How does it come to pass that so great a king . . . thus deprives himself of so many hearts that would have loved him and so many arms that would have served him?" It was not until December 1789, in the spirit of liberty of the French Revolution, that the National Assembly emancipated the Protestants; also the Sephardic Jews in 1790, originally from the Iberian Peninsula, and the Ashkenazic Jews from central and eastern Europe in 1791.

In 1807, Emperor Napoleon convened a Sanhedrin, a group of seventy-one Jewish leaders and rabbis charged with refining and codifying laws for the religious needs of the Jewish community that would not conflict with French law. A consistory and a synagogue, both responsible for maintaining the delicate balance, were established for each French department in which at least two thousand Jews lived. Thus the two branches of Judaism were united. No longer a nation within a nation, the Jews now were subject to the legal constraints of France. The Sanhedrin simulated the supreme judicial and religious council in ancient Palestine that ended with the destruction of the Second Temple in Jerusalem by the Roman general Titus in 70 A.D.

Bibliothèque nationale de France

A regally robed Napoleon holds a document, "Laws Given to Moses," on this allegorical painting, signifying his plan to integrate Jews into French society. The Jewish community, here offering allegiance to the emperor, is represented by a rabbi in black and kneeling elders (left) and a seated woman in white holding the tablet of the Ten Commandments (right), with religious symbols behind her. A Jewish prayer of 1807 asked that divine protection be granted to the worthy, powerful, and sincere Napoleon, "May his glory shine."

With citizenship and religious freedom, French Jews quickly achieved stature in professions once barred to them, such as finance, law, teaching, public office, and the military. It was the Dreyfus affair a century later that illustrated the underlying anti-Semitism harbored by right-wing French writers and political and religious groups during the Third Republic.

Alfred Dreyfus was a Jewish army captain, who had been falsely convicted of passing classified military documents to the Germans in 1894. He spent four years confined to the penal colony on Devil's Island in French Guiana and suffered the indignity of two unsuccessful trials in Paris to clear his name. During the trials, the city was torn between those eager to condemn the Jew Dreyfus and the Dreyfusards, those willing to stand up for justice and his acquittal. Emile Zola's courageous newspaper editorial of 1898, *"J'accuse,"* addressed to Félix Faure, president of the republic, was an indictment against the military and political authorities who originally acquitted the real traitor in the crime – the French officer Major Ferdinand Esterhazy. In 1906, twelve years later, in view of the overwhelming evidence of his innocence, Dreyfus finally was reinstated in the army as squadron chief, and designated a Chevalier of the Legion of Honor.

A crucified Dreyfus is tormented by General Auguste Mercier, the war minister responsible for his conviction, who thrusts a sponge soaked in vinegar to quench his thirst, on this India ink drawing by H.G. Ibels inscribed to the Dreyfusard writer and statesman Joseph Reinach. The scene recalls the cruel bystander who offered the same to the suffering Jesus on the cross (Matthew 27:48). Mercier was one of the military men accused by Emile Zola of being an accomplice to "one of the most iniquitous acts of this century."

One personal meeting told a story that paralleled many thousands of others during World War II. In the fall of 1967, a Swiss friend I had met in Zurich called to ask a favor. She now was living in Scarsdale, as her husband was a medical resident at a New York hospital. When she phoned, she was vacationing in Bern to visit her parents. Her uncle was alone in Paris where he had lived for decades. His wife recently died, and his three married daughters were living in other cities. They were busy with their own families, and their visits to Paris were infrequent. I agreed to meet him in a conveniently located hotel on the rue Rivoli, spend an hour or so talking with him, and, as expected, invite him for dinner some evening at his convenience.

We met at two in the afternoon, ordered Perriers, and began an interesting conversation. Jean was an elegant man in his late sixties, a civil engineer by profession, from which he was now retired. The invitation to dinner was extended for the following Friday.

My major interest was how his parents had adjusted to life in France, since he said that originally they came from Poland to the land of "Liberty, Equality, Fraternity" after the pogroms in the 1880s, which also had broken out in Russia and Romania. They were convinced that it would be futile to remain. In France Jews were not turned away. One-fifth of the immigrants in Paris were from eastern Europe. A new life began, as it had for the 1.65 million who settled in the United States at about that time and under the same circumstances. Jean and his younger brother were born in France. They were grateful to be here.

Jean's family would soon confront reality both from stories of the Dreyfus trial and later living through the roundup of Jews at the Velodrome d'Hiver in 1942. The roundup had been preceded in 1940-41 by Vichy's Jewish laws, the *Statut des Juifs*. They defined who was a Jew by ancestry and excluded them from employment in public administration, government, teaching, and all branches of the media and the army in France, Algeria, and all protectorates. No one was exempt. Guy de Rothschild, of the famous moneyed family, wrote in his memoir, *The Whims of Fortune*, "Under the surface of the social privileges from which I'd benefited since the day I was born, I could be nothing more than just another Jew." It recalled the statement of Dreyfus after the guilty verdict at his trial, "My only crime is to have been born a Jew."

Although Jean was proud that Jews had held high places in politics, they also had been affected by the *Statut des Juifs*. The Socialist prime minister Léon Blum, who served from 1936-37, had been deported to a German concentration camp by the Vichy government in 1942 and only freed three years later by U.S. troops. Pierre Mendès-France, prime minister from 1954-55, escaped Vichy imprisonment, fled to England, and joined the Free French forces as a pilot.

92

Among his own war stories, Jean told me of his brother, who was put on a transport going east during the Jewish roundup. In a daring attempt to flee his captives, he jumped from the moving train, running through the woods to safety. He was the only one on the train who survived the fate of the death camps. Jean joined the Resistance and lived in hiding during France's occupation from 1940 to 1944. Although they were assimilated, members of his family died in extermination camps. According to Jean, Vichy was an aberration, an occupied regime trying to exist without being destroyed. He remained proud of France, his country for good or ill.

After the war, Marshal Philippe Pétain and Pierre Laval, respectively premier and head of the Vichy government during Germany's occupation, were brought to trial. Laval was sentenced to death by firing squad in 1945. His last words were *"Vive la France!"* Pétain, called by de Gaulle a "great man, ruined by ambition and age," was confined to a fortress-prison off the French Atlantic coast. He died in 1951 at the age of ninety-five. De Gaulle accused both men of lacking any "sense of state."

Jean was not a religious man, but the story of his family's immigration to a more tolerant France resonated in the Neuilly synagogue we attended. The congregants, mainly Ashkenazim from eastern France or central and eastern Europe, worshipped in an atmosphere of deep sincerity and spirituality. The French-born rabbi, a painfully reticent man, was nevertheless a passionate patriot. After unsuccessfully trying to get to London to join the Free French, he made contact with the Resistance, was caught and condemned to death by the Germans, then freed by a French unit and participated at the end of the war in the liberation of various cities. The cantor, originally from Romania, was an opera singer with a voice that raised the level of traditional melodies to soaring heights. He saw military service during World War II and was commended by his regiment for courage under fire. The English-speaking president of the synagogue, a Holocaust survivor, was Advisor in Foreign Trade for France. He had been honored as a Chevalier of the Legion of Honor. In June 1969, he accepted our invitation to be the godfather of our eight-day-old son, Andrew.

The synagogue had seen its share of wars and dislocations. We never were invited by anyone in the congregation, as newcomers generally are in America, where a family feeling often prevails and committees compete for volunteers. We entered, we left, we wished members well with whom we met briefly. It reflected their guarded approach to strangers, which the wars in France had wrought. We were just an American family passing through that one day would depart and leave no friends behind. Since school was in session at the Cours Montaigne on Saturdays, there was no opportunity to attend services with the children. The one exception – a special prayer at the start of the Six-Day War.

A look at French history revealed one important difference with religious freedom in America. According to Arthur Hertzberg in his book *French Enlightenment and the Jews,* in the spirit of Napoleon's Civil Code and the new order, the law must give Jews French citizenship "in return for their agreement to perform their civic duty." This resulted in a forfeit of religious commitment, often leading to assimilation, if a conflict arose between secular and religious obligations. The granting of citizenship in America had no such restrictions that would limit freedom of worship. France's modern secularism, based on separation of church and state, originated with the French Revolution in order to strengthen national unity. This separation became law in 1905. It was bound to be contentious as the steady influx of Muslims from North Africa was changing the religious demographics of France.

The blending of two religious experiences began in the Neuilly synagogue (above) when Sephardic Jews, mainly from Algeria, arrived in metropolitan France after their homeland gained its independence from French control in 1962. The newly arrived, French-speaking Sephardim, who had held French citizenship since 1870, gave a burst of energy to the Ashkenazic congregants, many from other European countries, and who lived through the horrors of Nazi occupation.

94

[VII]
1968: THE DAYS OF MAY
STRIKES AND RIOTS

If, as we read in Zurich, the end of 1962 was more peaceful in the world than at any time in nearly thirty years, then 1968 was the least peaceful. The escalating Vietnam War had sparked student protests in universities all over the world. In France came the Days of May, which actually lasted to the middle of June. There were not only student strikes that began at the University of Nanterre, ten miles west of Paris, and spread to the Sorbonne in Paris but also massive sit-ins and demonstrations of industrial workers. Soviet Russia's grip on its eastern bloc countries was making them restive, especially in Czechoslovakia, with its attempt to democratize its brand of socialism. Soviet tanks rolled into Prague in August in order to stop Czech liberalization.

In America, the Reverend Dr. Martin Luther King Jr. was killed on April 4. The nonviolent movement was over. Black ghettos erupted in fury in major cities. On April 23, student radicals at Columbia University occupied five buildings, including the president's office, originally opposing both a consortium of universities that was conducting research for the military and also the construction of a gymnasium on public land in Harlem without community agreement. The police were called in a few days later. On May 1, the school shut down completely. Students who were not on strike condemned the radicals for trampling on their rights to attend classes. Robert Kennedy, then a Democratic candidate for president, died on June 6 from an assassin's bullet after winning the California primary. His opposition to the unpopular Vietnam War was silenced, but his message grew louder. We began to think that America was going mad. One college professor stated ironically that these dire events raised the popularity of such men as Charles de Gaulle whose strong leadership maintained national order. But in France all hell was breaking loose. De Gaulle had lost control.

On March 22, student agitators strongly opposed to the Vietnam War at the University of Nanterre demanded that five of their comrades be freed who were arrested for blowing out windows of American companies. These student *enragés,* or the angry ones, were led by Daniel Cohn-Bendit, a red-headed sociology student, called "Danny the Red," of German-Jewish parentage. The *New York Times* described the anarchist *enragés* as being of "Trotskyite persuasions." A psychology professor from Nanterre, writing in the magazine *Paris Match,* documented the underlying problem. He wrote that Nanterre had about 3,500 students in 1966. Two years later there were 12,000. He had 80 students in his classes and knew them all. He now had 400. Contacts with them were completely reduced. When the dean closed down the university on May 2, the *enragés* then moved on to the Sorbonne, itself ripe for revolt. The complaints there were similar. One professor had a class of 1,700. His only personal contact with them, he said, was "jostling with them in the halls."

Traditionally, a French university education was open to all lycée students who passed the qualifying *baccalauréat*, a much more difficult version of the American precollege SAT exams. An enormous increase in general university enrollment occurred, a growth from 175,000 in 1958 to 500,000 in 1968. The results were overcrowded, outdated facilities, and often a teacher shortage. Also, the rigorous studies that once would have placed students among the elite only guaranteed that they would be part of a huge mass of graduates, especially in the humanities, with no certainty of employment. Ruthless exams, called "sudden death," determined if they remained, had to repeat the year, or left. The dropout rate after the first year was recorded as high as 50 percent.

Things went from bad to worse. On May 4, the Sorbonne was shut down, only the second time in its seven-hundred-year history. The New Left student-power movement demanded control of the university administration and the violent overthrow of the "capitalist establishment." Four students had been arrested. Three days later, more than 10,000 students took to the streets demanding their release. On the so-called Night of the Barricades alone, May 10-11, at the height of the rioting, more than 350 were wounded. Barricades were erected, constructed of ripped-up paving stones, trees, wooden planks, and whatever could be found to halt the specially trained riot police, the CRS *(Compagnies Républicaines de Sécurité)*. Grenades exploded; tear gas filled the air; parked cars were in flames; windows were smashed. The writer Janet Flanner claimed that Paris might not have fallen in June 1940 if the young French soldiers had fought the Germans with the same spirit as the Left Bank rioters.

Returning from a trip to Afghanistan on May 11, Prime Minister Georges Pompidou appeased the students by reopening the Sorbonne and freeing the jailed students. On May 13, the labor unions called a general strike. Paris was almost paralyzed. The timing could not have been worse. The Paris peace talks between the representatives of North Vietnam and the United States were underway at the Hotel Majestic near the Arc de Triomphe. De Gaulle would have preferred a more congenial atmosphere in which to play host and enjoy the prestige of having the meetings in Paris.

While the Left Bank was burning, the atmosphere on the boulevard Jean Mermoz was tense. Philippe wanted to send us to his parents in Belgium during the strikes, given the possibility that rampaging university students might decide to invade Neuilly. He even had two jerry cans of gasoline at the ready in order to drive to Brussels. I appreciated his concern, but we were not leaving France. I expected that any rioting students preferred to air their grievances on their own turf – the Sorbonne and the boulevards of Saint-Michel and Saint-Germain. In Neuilly, there were no paving stones to dislodge from the streets and boulevards, no cars to burn, safely parked in their assigned spots in underground garages.

On May 14, de Gaulle left France on a state visit to Romania, urged by Prime Minister Pompidou to do what he did best – encourage the countries behind the Iron Curtain to end the artificial divisions of Eastern and Western blocs and proceed independently toward a union of Europe. He was greeted triumphantly by university students as a hero of Western democracy. We could not imagine an American president leaving such a scene of turmoil, but de Gaulle believed that "the chief of state should not be in the front line when things are at their hottest." He would act only after his ministers restored order. It was not the first time that de Gaulle departed a crisis in order to give the French a chance to cool off. Four days later, he cut short his state visit. No one was cooling off. On May 18, he returned, furiously rebuking his ministers, "De Gaulle has only to turn his back and everything collapses. Play time is over!"

My letter home, dated May 21, painted a dismal picture. But the post offices were on strike. A friend driving to Belgium promised to stamp and send it.

> We are beset with strikes – mail, metro, electricity, etc., by unions joining in sympathy with the students. Garbage is piled up high on the streets, no transportation, no gasoline. People are lined up in front of every food store in case this becomes a long strike. All staples, like spaghetti and potatoes, are being bought up and stores are cleaned out. The only thing I'm worried about is milk for the children, so I ran up to ANIC (the American commissary) and bought five boxes of Carnation powder and bottled water. No one knows when it will end. I also got a bottle of alcohol for the wick cooker for when the gas goes off, which is sure to come soon. Electricity, too, so I bought candles. No mail coming in or out of the post office. To get the allotted ten liters of gasoline per car, I joined the line with dozens of others, pushing our cars to the gas pumps in order to save a few drops of gasoline. There are also lines at banks, since withdrawals are being limited to five hundred francs a customer. Some Americans and British are stranded without being able to exchange their francs to get home. It's a mess!

Spontaneous carpools sprang up. I was driving Philippe to the office daily on the place de la Concorde while metro workers were on strike. We tried to pick people up along the way, calling out our destination to see if they wanted a lift. One afternoon, as I was driving down the boulevard de la Grande Armée to bring Philippe home, I saw a young woman on foot who looked like she was headed toward Paris. I opened the window and yelled, "Place de la Concorde." She thought I was asking directions. *"Tout droit"* (straight ahead), she said. I left it at that, rather than hold up the long line of cars behind me.

Another incident, memorable to say the least, occurred on our way home. The official numbers were that every night at 6 P.M., seventy thousand cars were driven to work by Parisians who, under normal conditions, refused to use public transportation. That night, due to the strikes, it seemed that all seventy thousand had converged on the porte des Ternes, which led to the avenue du Roule, our usual route home to Neuilly. Total deadlock.

Horns began to blow in an ungodly, claxonlike noise. Impatient French drivers, prone to anarchy behind the wheel anyway, got out of their cars to see if there was a gendarme to break up the jam. No gendarme. After a half-hour, Philippe, whose idea of heaven is driving alone on a six-lane highway, could stand it no longer. He got out of the car, walked to the west end of the circle, and began to direct traffic inch by inch. He motioned to the left, a car moved an inch. He motioned to the right, a car moved another inch. Inch by inch and forty-five minutes later, the logjam broke. Cars began to move. Cheers and applause rose from the open windows of the cars for my hero, the traffic director.

By May 23, ten million union workers were on strike in almost every facet of French life, joining in the spirit of the student demonstrations for their own reasons of pay raises and improved working conditions. The Socialist François Mitterrand, thinking that de Gaulle was finished, seized the chance to succeed him and called upon Pierre Mendès-France to be his prime minister. De Gaulle was not resigning. Paris in the spring, glorified in song, must have been unforgettable to Sargent Shriver, brother-in-law of John F. Kennedy, as he presented his credentials to President de Gaulle as the new U.S. ambassador.

On May 29, de Gaulle, who found the situation "incomprehensible" and "a terrible shock," flew to the French army base in Baden-Baden to meet with General Jacques Massu, then commander of French forces in Germany. No one knew where he was. Again we wondered how a president could leave his country in chaos, this time without a trace. He returned a day later, energized and determined to deal with the strikers. In a radio address, he called for the nation to support him, blamed the situation on the Communists, and hinted that force would be used. A pro-de Gaulle demonstration of half a million people walked up the Champs-Elysées, reflecting their fears of the consequences if the situation continued. The agitator, Daniel Cohn–Bendit, was expelled from France and sent back to Germany. The chants of right-wing marchers among the demonstrators, "France for the French," and "Cohn-Bendit to Dachau," exposed their xenophobia and latent anti-Semitism.

The man of the hour was Prime Minister Georges Pompidou. In addition to his concessions to the students, he and his ministers negotiated endlessly through long hours of the night with union representatives and employers. Pay raises and benefits were hammered out, but among the demands not granted was the freedom to organize. Union members called a general strike, which lasted into June. At the Sorbonne, with the promise of increased communication between students and professors, input into academic decisions through elected student bodies, and improved teaching facilities, the student strikes petered out. The Sorbonne and the Odéon theater, which the students had occupied, were cleaned of the detritus they left behind. The burnt shells of cars, often part of the barricades, were removed, and the ripped-up streets eventually repaved.

Le Canard Enchâiné claimed that the problem with Gaullist cabinet ministers was that their interests were solely those of President de Gaulle and not those of the people. The minister of education misjudged the cause of the Left Bank riots, and the interior minister let the police take control of the rioting and then blamed the students for the ensuing chaos.

Tous à genoux ! Le Quartier Latin est repavé de bonnes intentions.

"Everyone on your knees! The Latin Quarter is repaved with good intentions."
Moisan. *Le Canard Enchâiné,* May 15, 1968

Prime Minister Georges Pompidou, the arbiter between the government, the unions, and students here distributes paving stones to Gaullist ministers to repair the torn-up streets on the Left Bank. A security policeman stands guard (left) while nearby a bystander describes Pompidou as a man who favors a no-holds-barred dialogue. Unusually calm students in the rear watch the repaving. Above them is the spire of the Saint-Germain-des-Près church, a silent witness to the violence on the Left Bank boulevards in which more than two thousand civilians and police were hurt.

100

THE DAYS OF MAY – A RETROSPECTIVE

In his "Letter to Young People," dated December 14, 1897, Emile Zola, champion of justice in the Dreyfus affair, encouraged the youth of France always to follow their consciences in the greater cause of truth and honor. His advice seemed as appropriate then as in 1968, when students on the Left Bank went on strike to improve university conditions and to realize their hopes for a better future. Excerpts from Zola's letter capture his impassioned idealism:

Where are you going, you young men, you bands
of students who dash through the streets,
demonstrating angrily or enthusiastically,
obeying the irresistible urge to express in
public what your indignant consciences feel?. . .
    Oh, when I was young myself, the Latin Quarter
I knew throbbed with the proud passions of
youth, with . . . hatred of the brute strength
that crushes minds and wrings souls dry.

In the days of the Second Empire, I watched the Latin Quarter play its courageous role of opposition, unjustly sometimes but always out of an excess of unfettered human freedom. The Latin Quarter . . . jeered teachers whose courses it found suspect, and rose up against anyone who was visibly on the side of darkness and despotism. In that Quarter burned the sacred flame, the splendid folly that inhabits twenty–year-olds, so certain that all hopes will be realized and that tomorrow will bring the triumph of the ideal City. . . .

Whenever the Latin Quarter was reported to be ablaze with passion, you could be sure of what was behind that: an outburst of some juvenile love of justice, scorning compromise, spurred by heartfelt enthusiasm. And how spontaneous it all was, how they flowed through the streets, like a river at the flood! . . .

Youth, be always on the side of justice. . . . Who will stand up and demand justice be done – if not you?. . . If you do not take the most sublime of risks, if you do not launch into a superb and perilous cause, if you do not stand up to an entire nation in the name of ideal justice, then who will?. . .

Where are you going, you young men, you students, you twenty-year-olds who dash about the streets, demonstrating, voicing your gallantry and hope in the midst of our discord?

'We're going to the aid of humanity, truth and justice!'

The Dreyfus Affair ©CNRS Editions, Paris 1994
English translation © Eleanor Levieux 1996, courtesy Yale University Press

At Prime Minister Georges Pompidou's insistence and against his own wishes, President de Gaulle agreed that the National Assembly should be dissolved and new elections held. The date was set for June 23 and 30. Its mandate would be to restore order to France. Reacting against the turmoil of the strikes, the voters, in a wave of pro-de Gaulle support, gave the Gaullists an overwhelming win of 358 out of the new 487-seat Assembly.

FORTE POUSSEE GAULLISTE

Escaro. *Le Canard Enchâiné,* June 26, 1968

A "Strong Gaullist Push" gave President de Gaulle's political party a huge victory in the June National Assembly elections following the devastating strikes and riots of May. The Gaullists feared that his defeat would be as dangerous for France, seen as the symbolic Marianne, her Phrygian cap flying, as if he had pushed her over a cliff. De Gaulle still had looming problems to solve – inadequate university facilities, labor unrest, unemployment, rising prices, and a weakened franc.

102

Buoyed by the results, de Gaulle began to reshuffle his cabinet in order to implement his policies more efficiently. "Regionalization," or decentralization of authority, and "participation" were the keywords of his referendum, planned for a vote the following year. Prime Minister Pompidou did not believe the concept to be entirely workable. We were shocked when de Gaulle replaced Pompidou with Maurice Couve de Murville, who had served as foreign minister for six years. Even though de Gaulle had told Pompidou to settle the strikes "at whatever price," he faulted him for mishandling the situation by giving the students a free hand and alienating them by neglecting his idea of participating in the decision-making process. De Gaulle's excuse for replacing Pompidou was that the prime minister was tired and needed a long vacation, the better to prepare himself for the mandate that the nation one day would entrust to him. Having accomplished hard-won terms with the labor unions, for his pains Pompidou now was an ex-prime minister. But at least he was considered to be the dauphin, the Gaullist heir apparent of France, waiting to take his place as president.

As for the discontented labor force, the underlying economic problems of France already had been described a year before the Days of May in the runaway best seller *Le Défi Américain, (The American Challenge)*, by Jean-Jacques Servan-Schreiber, the French journalist and publisher of *l'Express,* the weekly news magazine. Four hundred thousand copies of his book were sold throughout Europe in the first twelve weeks of publication. I bought a copy at Brentano's after it was translated into English. How often would there be a book written by a Frenchman, admitting that America had something to teach the French, something that would be to their advantage?

Servan-Schreiber's observations about the industrial needs of France were on target, but there was one prediction involving American power that struck us as unimaginable in 1968. Could it happen? He wrote that if the Soviet Union ever ceased to be its main rival and the United States lost the stimulation and restraint that comes from competition, it would be dangerous both for America and the world. His premise, "A nation holding a monopoly of power would look on imperialism as a kind of duty, and would take its own success as proof that the rest of the world should follow its example." His solution – a strong, technologically united Europe to serve as a buffer to America as the sole power in the world. The Common Market was a start, although de Gaulle felt that supranational bodies reduced the powers of the individual state to act in its own best interests, or, as he stated, "to be masters in our own house."

National traits came into play as Servan-Schreiber analyzed the strikes that ravaged France in May. The French assumed that men were hostile, selfish, and skeptical of human potential. The resultant "legal straitjacket quite naturally inhibits change." No problems were resolved without permission from a superior, and since 50 percent of France's total output came from nationalized industries in which decision making was bureaucratically slow, he often did not know what the government's policy was in his particular area. The fear of delegating authority debilitated the economy. Risks were avoided.

On the other hand, he added, American young people were educated to think and problem solve. America's strengths were organization, management, and investment in research estimated at three times that of Europe. The latter led to scientific discovery, resulting in accelerated technological improvement. Industry, government, and the university worked as a team in a process of creative cross-fertilization, not in the individualistic French way. He described America as "Europe with a 15-year head start."

Then there was John D'Gerolamo, our neighbor in the garden apartment downstairs. John was Director of Administration for Europe, Africa, and the Middle East for IBM, the multinational company on the place de la Madeleine. It was a big title for this modest, brilliant man from Louisiana who took great pride in his family – four children and his wife, Joan.

One Sunday, John was getting ready for a trip to Italy. IBM was sending him to participate in a T-Group of European business leaders to discuss ways to sharpen their skills as corporation heads. We assumed *T* meant training. Servan-Schreiber noted that the French subsidiary of IBM spent 10 percent of its total payroll on expanding the proficiency of its personnel. "This wager on man," he wrote, "is the origin of America's new dynamism."

The T-Group experience, as reported by John when he returned a week later, was intense, really mind-expanding. Three-hour meetings were held in the mornings and afternoons. Every possible problem that department heads experienced was discussed and solutions hammered out together. It was typical of how American firms educate their management personnel. John's only complaint was that nobody invited him to the spontaneous, individual cocktail parties in the evening. "But," he admitted, "they all came to mine." We assured him that this was a sign of his leadership quality. Some of those attending might have thought it presumptuous to invite an IBM director, unassuming though he was. John appreciated the T-Group experience and its business-efficient proposals, regardless of the cocktail invitations.

A few days later, he and Joan went out to dinner with his IBM colleagues, as they often had done before. The camaraderie and cooperation of American business people abroad made the difference to the success of their work. It carried over to the corporate wives who enjoyed socializing at the comfort level of familiar language, backgrounds, and sharing experiences far from home.

When President de Gaulle was asked his opinion of *Le Défi Américain,* he supposedly replied in confidence that he thought the analysis was sound but the solutions were weak. His way of addressing the challenge of America's business infiltration of Europe was to declare war on the dollar. In a press conference in 1965, de Gaulle had pushed for a return to the gold standard as the basis for international payments. His policy was to convert a large amount of France's dollar currency reserves to gold, which he stated, "does not change its nature." Some called his obsession with gold his second *force de frappe.* At issue was the $40 billion balance of payments deficit owed by the U.S. to foreign creditors over a seventeen-year period, due in great part to the costs of the Vietnam War, American occupation forces, economic and military aid abroad, and the buying up of European companies. Since the dollar was a privileged reserve currency that had the same value as gold, maintained at $35 an ounce, the U.S. could print more dollars to settle its international debts rather than backing them with gold. De Gaulle complained that America was exporting inflation.

European and American economists were not enthusiastic about de Gaulle's plan, believing it to be more political than realistic, just one more of his attempts to remove France and Europe from America's influence. Since all major currencies were tied to the dollar, if there was a major problem with its stability, European countries would cooperate with the U.S. to solve it. What we did see in Paris was a scarcity of American tourists. Not only were they irked with de Gaulle's attack on the dollar, but President Johnson had asked that all non-essential travel abroad be deferred as part of his national austerity program.

The Days of May passed. There were immediate economic aftershocks. Prices rose due to closed factories and a fall in production, the pay raises and benefits negotiated for the workers, and repairs to Left Bank properties. The franc was weakened. Inflation was imminent. Unemployment mounted. American investments in France were cut back. Try as he might to forestall the franc's devaluation, called by de Gaulle "the worst possible absurdity," it went into effect the following year after his defeat and our final departure from France. De Gaulle's gold war faded.

After the strikes, I wrote home, "I hope de Gaulle can calm things down until we leave next July. Then I'll be only too happy to read about this mess in the daily *New York Times* somewhere in New Jersey."

In August it rained every day. For the most part, we stayed indoors. Steven asked if God had an umbrella. I said no, it was God who made the rain. He replied "He's good at that." Paris in the spring was no joy, but the summer ended with a smile.

— **Retenez-moi un sculpteur, Malraux, et le Mont Blanc.**

"Reserve a sculptor for me, Malraux, and Mont Blanc"
Moisan. *Le Canard Enchâiné*. November 13, 1968

Riding on a wave of popularity after the May strikes with the Gaullist victory in the National Assembly, President de Gaulle is pictured standing on Mount Rushmore, inspired by the stone-carved faces of America's great presidents, with a nod to the departing Lyndon Baines Johnson (right). De Gaulle orders André Malraux, his minister of culture (behind him) to arrange for his likeness to be preserved on majestic Mont Blanc in southeastern France. Thus the Grand Charles – general, president, and defender of France's honor – would be memorialized for posterity.

[VIII]
1969: ENDINGS AND BEGINNINGS

Richard Nixon was America's new president. There was mutual respect between him and Charles de Gaulle that would assure warmer relations than those that existed with President Johnson. What we could not know after Nixon's inauguration in January 1969 was that President de Gaulle had only six months left in office. What we did know was that our days in France were coming to an end. We would be leaving in July, a month after our third child was born. We now would have three children, each born in a different country.

Before the June 1968 elections, Georges Pompidou had advised President de Gaulle not to risk including a referendum on decentralizing the decision-making powers of Paris bureaucrats in favor of newly created economic regions. It was the right advice. The negative reaction of the French voters to the May strikes had given the Gaullists a huge majority of seats in the new National Assembly. The loss of influence of the French Communists and leftist parties was compounded when the Soviets invaded Czechoslovakia two months later. Pompidou, now no longer prime minister, still held a seat in the National Assembly, thereby consolidating his political visibility and support for the future.

The higher wages that the workers had won after the Days of May were being cancelled out by higher prices. A general strike in mid-March 1969, called by its dissatisfied union leaders a "day of warning," was described by de Gaulle as bordering on treason. An editorial in the *International Herald Tribune* commented that the French president's "willingness to treat millions of his citizens with contempt is always startling."

Yet de Gaulle still believed it was essential for France's future to bring the previously delayed referendum to a vote. April 27, 1969, was the date set for the vote on the constitutional revision. The dual issues were decentralization and reform of the senate. His plan was to loosen the hold of the centralized government in Paris, or "de-Napoleonize France." The two questions on the ballot required a yes or no answer: "Do you favor regionalization?" and "Should the senate be transformed into a purely consultative assembly?" The first issue would give greater autonomy to the newly created, twenty-two regional governments (including Corsica), but left the voters confused as to what functions would be affected and who might lose existing benefits from the new arrangement. The second issue, according to its critics, would have turned the senate into an advisory body without a political role. Those who opposed his plan were called by de Gaulle in his luxuriant choice of words, "fanatics of destruction," "doctrinaires of negation," "specialists of demagogy." He stated that the results of the vote would determine whether he would continue with his mandate as chief of state or resign immediately. It was a decision he was not obliged to take. His elected term would have ended in 1972.

André Malraux thought the theme of the referendum was "absurd," merely an attempt to reassure de Gaulle of France's confidence in him. The French, uneasy about the consequences of decentralization and an ineffective senate, turned it down by a percentage margin of 53 no to 47 yes votes. De Gaulle announced that his function as president of the republic would end at noon on April 28, the day after the failed vote. His personal papers were packed up at the Elysée and carted to his home, La Boisserie, in Colombey-les-Deux-Eglises.

"The Grand Army of those who support me?"
« La Grande Armé de ceux qui me soutiennent » (de Gaulle)

« Il neigeait... »

"It was snowing"
Moisan. *Le Canard Enchâiné,* April 30, 1969

Charles de Gaulle, portrayed on horseback as a despondent Napoleon, and his Grand Army of wounded ministers are being led to their encampment in Colombey-les-Deux-Eglises by Georges Pompidou (right) who succeeded to the presidency in mid-June. They are pelted with a snowstorm of *NON*, representing more than the million no votes that defeated de Gaulle's April referendum. He had taken a political risk. He lost. The scene recalls Napoleon's defeats in Moscow in 1812 and at Waterloo in 1815 when he wrote, "Everything failed me just when everything had succeeded!"

On April 30, my letter home, written in a state of fatigue, oversimplified the reasons for the failed referendum, but not the reactions of the people:

> France is in a state of shock. They never really meant to throw the old man out, but he almost begged to have his bluff called. This time the French did it. Being defeated on a referendum like this is like Nixon resigning on the issue of confidence if an interstate transportation bill he supported was not approved by the voters. De Gaulle didn't have to stake his career on such a referendum, but he over-did "me or chaos" once too often. Now nobody knows why, and they don't know what's coming next. Everyone is walking around with their tail between their legs in Paris wishing they could vote over again. De Gaulle is in his country home brooding and won't see anyone or give any statement. He certainly stabilized France, but someone like Pompidou could carry on the domestic policies and do better on the foreign scene as far as relations with America and Great Britain are concerned.

At La Boisserie de Gaulle was serene. He was sure that "when they wake up, they will no doubt see that I was right." He would write his memoirs. There would be long walks in the neighboring parks and forests of Colombey-les-Deux-Eglises. He would travel – first to Ireland, where his maternal relatives originated; then later to the Escorial in Madrid, which he had never visited; and to China to visit Mao. Visitors to La Boisserie described de Gaulle as more tranquil than he had ever been, ensconced in what he once described as his "melancholy woods and meadows, old mountains, and unpretentious villages where nothing has changed for thousands of years." Madame de Gaulle agreed, "The general is happy now."

Claude Mauriac, his secretary for many years, once called de Gaulle "one who really believes himself to be among those responsible for our planet's future." Upon completing his memoir *Salvation,* which covered events in the years 1944 to 1946, de Gaulle did contemplate the planet, also his country, and old age. He wrote poetically, facing his mortality:

> This is my home. In the tumult of men and events, solitude was my
>   temptation, now it is my friend. What other satisfaction can be
>   sought once you have confronted history? . . . life wages a battle
>   it has never lost. . . . I find consolation in her wisdom. . . .
>   As age triumphs, nature comes closer to me. . . .
> Old Earth, worn by the ages, wracked by rain and storm, exhausted
>   yet ever ready to produce what life must have to go on!
> Old France, weighed down with history, prostrated by wars and
>   revolutions, endlessly vacillating from greatness to decline, but
>   revived, century after century, by the genius of renewal!
> Old man, exhausted by ordeal, detached from human deeds,
>   feeling the approach of the eternal cold, but always watching
>   in the shadows for the gleam of hope.

As we were packing on a Sunday morning in early June, I asked Debby if she would remember the Eiffel Tower when we got back to America.

Debby (four years old): "I don't like the Eiffel Tower."

Steven (five and a half): "Then don't remember it."

But there were many things that I would remember. Seeing one's country from a distance did wonders for tempering ingrained nationalism. Growing up in a foreign land and language would develop strengths in Steven and Debby that they could bank on for the future. Self-sufficiency was one of them. Before they attended the Cours Montaigne and in the absence of television, the two had an enviable sibling closeness, amusing themselves with stories or word plays of their own creation. Prime Minister Pompidou was "Pompy," and the sound of the police siren as it cleared the streets for daily emergencies was "pampom." During our last year, with the pregnancy, when I needed my afternoon rest on doctor's orders and with Steven at school after lunch, Debby would play alone in her room for an hour and a half, talking to her doll, or looking at pictures in her French books. *Nicolas* and *Pimprenelle* were her favorites, those wide-eyed children, he in his blue-striped, monogrammed pajamas, and she in her pink-checked nightgown, or the adventures of another boy and girl, *Sylvain and Sylvette,* outwitting four wily animals: a bear, a boar, a fox, and a wolf. The stories of Tintin, the young adventurer, once referred to by de Gaulle as "my only international rival," and Babar, the royal elephant, were saved for bedtimes.

I enjoyed the lilting French greeting of *"Bon Jour, Madame,"* be it from salesgirls, shopkeepers, or farmers at the twice-weekly, open-air market in Neuilly. My replies never acquired the same musical intonations. One custom of tipping the butcher at Christmas time was a lesson learned the hard way. Not realizing the tradition, I was ignored by the butcher on the rue des Huissiers one year for not giving him the expected gratuity. Another butcher had to be found. He would benefit from my mistake at the next holiday season.

Two writings involving a mixture of French and English were favorites. The first was Art Buchwald's column explaining Thanksgiving to the French, reprinted each November in the *International Herald Tribune.* It was called "Le Jour de Merci Donnant" (the Day of Thanks Giving). The familiar cast included Miles Standish (Kilomètres Deboutish) [*kilomètres* = miles, *debout* = stand(ish)], John Alden, and Priscilla Mullens (no translation). The Pilgrims sailed to the New World where they landed at Plymouth (a *voiture américaine*) [an American car]. Thus the story unfolded with bilingual wit. Buchwald concluded that thanks to Kilomètres Deboutish, "Thanksgiving was the only time that American families eat better than the French." The second were children's cartoon books, featuring Asterix the Gaul (the English version). The stories took place in 50 B.C., when Caesar's legionnaires occupied all of Gaul except for a little village in the northwest corner of the country led by the feisty Asterix in his winged hat, who had superhuman strength thanks to a secret potion provided by the venerable druid, Getafix. Obelix, an enormous man with braided hair, was Asterix's partner in fighting the Romans. Other inhabitants included Vitalstatistix, the village chief, and Cacafonix the bard, whose off-key singing definitely was to be avoided. The Romans had names such as Gluteus Maximus, Marcus Ginandtonicus, Magnumopus, and Crismus Bonus.

Our best souvenir from France was Andrew, born on the first day of summer at 4:30 A.M. The birds had begun to chirp outside the window of the American Hospital, and there he was, robust and beautiful. My fears during my nine months had been for naught, like babysitting for a friend's child who came down with German measles a week later, or having a tooth x-rayed without the obligatory lead apron. Steven's *onzième* class teacher wrote a dear note, here translated:

> Mademoiselle Viè, and the little children of the 11*ème*, share the joy of
> Steven and his parents. They rejoice in the happy arrival of the little
> brother to whom they wish wisdom and health. Each send him a kiss.

Wisdom (*sagesse*) also meant good behavior. It would be interesting to see if Andrew would be as disciplined in America as Steven and Debby, who had been molded in their earliest years by French schooling. Andrew remained *sage* and smiling.

Steven's final report card said he was becoming a child who applied himself. And so he was. Debby won first prize in mischief, just as Steven had done in the *jardin d'enfants* at the same age. Perhaps it was the cultural difference between American and French youngsters. Or perhaps it was just mine. "She wants to learn to read," her teacher wrote, almost scoffing at such a concept for a four-year-old. The report ended, "Her good humor and smile should make her dynamic." And so they did.

On Sunday, July 20, eight days after we arrived in America, the Apollo 11 spacecraft landed on the moon. Civilian commander Neil Armstrong and Colonel Edwin (Buzz) Aldrin of the Air Force took their first steps on its powdery surface. *Paris Match* reported, "In 88 hours and 50 minutes, their eyes would open on another world . . . other men soon would follow in their footsteps on the moon."

Vietnam, race riots, college unrest – all momentarily were forgotten. America had kept President Kennedy's promise, "This is a new ocean, and I believe that the U.S. must sail on it." Viewing the Earth, Neil Armstrong described it as "big and bright and beautiful." It was exactly how we saw it. We were home.

C'EST LA LUNE FINALE !

ATROCE NATURE — Il ne sait pas encore bien où il met les pieds.

"He still does not know what he's getting into."
Moisan. *Le Canard Enchâiné,* July 16, 1969

On the same day that the American astronauts soared to the moon, Georges Pompidou, now president of France, was satirized as a space hero in astronaut gear (center) adorned with the sash and medallions of office. His lunar module resembles a royal throne. He walks carefully on craters harboring weird moon creatures. Charles de Gaulle is a craggy formation on the moon's surface (left), his silhouette blowing off atomic steam through his general's hat, a hint of his antagonism towards the more pragmatic Georges Pompidou, as is the quote (above). In his retirement, de Gaulle would refer to "poor Pompidou," who now must deal with such lingering issues as university and labor reforms, removing censorship from French television news, and the worst blows to de Gaulle's policies – devaluing the franc and reconsidering Great Britain's entry into the Common Market. To Pompidou, the presidency was as isolated as the "atrocious" moonscape. He complained, "To think that I can't even go for a short walk about Paris!" At home in La Boisserie, de Gaulle was intent on finishing his *Memoirs of Hope,* detailing his presidential years. He died suddenly on November 9, 1970, a month after the first volume was published to wide acclaim. President Pompidou declared, "France is a widow." De Gaulle was remembered as a strong leader, often at odds with America, but firmly convinced that his was the way to a more peaceful world.

Epilogue

THEN AND NOW

Four decades after the 1960s, many things in our two European countries of residence and in America have changed, some for better, some for worse. Their roots can be traced back to that watershed time.

In 2002, the neutral Switzerland we once knew had adapted to new realities, finally joining the United Nations, one of forty-seven countries to have been elected to its Human Rights Council based in Geneva. The Swiss also approved of joining the European Union's passport-free zone and increasing its security cooperation with other nations to deal with cross-border terrorists and organized crime.

Closure finally came to Paul Grüninger, the St. Gallen police chief convicted in 1940 of falsifying entry documents before World War II for thousands of refugees fleeing the Nazis. In 1995, he was vindicated by the city government. It stated that although it could not change the decision reached at his trial, the conflict between his civic duties and humanitarian instincts was officially recognized.

The original Swiss sympathy for the refugees turned to resentment years after the war when Holocaust survivors or family members attempted to retrieve dormant Swiss bank accounts. The honorary president of the Union Bank of Switzerland called it a "conspiracy to take over the world's financial markets." After a class action suit filed in Brooklyn, U.S. local and state government threats to stop doing business with Swiss banks, and endless deliberations, a settlement of $1.25 billion was arranged in August 1998. The monetary divisions were to be worked out by the parties involved.

In France, the spirit of Charles de Gaulle still hovered over the country as the new president, Nicolas Sarkozy, was determined to restore Gaullist energy, reform, and pride. Two events that de Gaulle championed have come to pass: French nuclear power is well underway and Germany and Vietnam now are united countries. But, while de Gaulle ordered NATO to leave France in 1966, Sarkozy announced in 2009 that it was time to rejoin as a full member for the defense of France and Europe. National interests had determined France's decision to keep out of the Iraq War, based mainly on previous, traumatic losses in colonial Algeria and Vietnam. No nation, Sarkozy declared, can prevail militarily in a country not its own. Also, when France and Holland, both original members of the Common Market, voted against the European Union's constitution in May 2005, it was their fear of unemployment due to an influx of cheap labor from newly admitted Eastern European countries. France's 10 percent unemployment was the only reality the voters understood.

In 1967, President de Gaulle predicted that Israel's success in the Six-Day War would foment "frantic agitation" in the region. On the fortieth anniversary of the war, the media described it as a "wasted victory," referring to two intifadas, a war with Hezbollah in 2006, frequent Hamas rocket attacks from Gaza into Israel, and Israeli counterattacks. After the Gaza confrontation in late December 2008, a special American envoy was sent to the Middle East to observe and report back to the president on how to find the allusive peace.

As President de Gaulle once warned America of being the world's policeman, a similar alarm was sounded by Jean-Jacques Servan-Schreiber, who wrote of the danger if it ever became the sole superpower without the restraint of competition, such as that of the USSR during the cold war. With the demise of the Soviet Union in 1991, it had happened. A U.S. military policy of preemptive war to vanquish communism in Vietnam or world terrorism in Iraq seemed contrary to American tradition. Anti-Americanism flourished abroad, especially in the current climate of ethnic populations striving for self-determination.

A current concern is a possible renewal of the cold war as Russia reacts strongly to NATO's expansion into Eastern European countries once in the Soviet orbit and also to Washington's previous plan to place missile defense systems in neighboring Poland and the Czech Republic. U.S. assurances that these were not meant for Russia but to meet threats from unpredictable countries like Iran, failed to convince the Kremlin. With its rich resources, Russia is capable of cutting off supplies of natural gas to its European clients, as it did in the Ukraine over payment disputes. Its incursion into Georgia in 2008 revived thoughts of the Soviet invasion of Czechoslovakia in 1968, causing anxiety in former Soviet bloc countries, as well as in the West.

In America, the historian Garry Wills wrote that regarding our awareness of the rights of others, "Much of what is good around us took its origin from that troubled and troubling period." Although President Lyndon Johnson knew that with the passage of civil rights laws the Democrats had lost the South, conscience followed legislation. After forty years, the perpetrators of the most horrific of racial crimes -- the Alabama church bombing that killed four young black girls, and the murder of three civil rights workers in Mississippi -- were caught and found guilty. The Voting Rights Act of 1965 was extended by Congress for twenty-five years and signed by President George W. Bush on July 17, 2006. A black senator from Illinois, Barak Obama, won the 2008 presidency as a Democrat, energizing voters, including those in southern states. President Johnson would have been encouraged for the future of the Democratic Party in the South. To what degree, only time would tell. The party's mandate now was to restore confidence nationally and America's reputation internationally. As John Kennedy used the technology of television to his advantage, so Barak Obama rallied millions of supporters on the Internet to work and raise funds for his campaign.

The results of the 2008 election were celebrated world wide, not only by those eager for the end to an unpopular administration, but also by minority populations who were euphoric that the new president had overcome racial barriers. It was a far cry from the church bombings and high-powered water hoses that were turned on civil rights demonstrators in the Alabama of the sixties. Rather, it was in the spirit of Martin Luther King Jr.'s 1959 speech in Hawaii, the birthplace of Barack Obama two years later, that the success of the civil rights movement would "free the soul of America." In France, minority leaders did not believe that it could happen there, regardless of her egalitarian policy. Candidates for high office were chosen within the political establishment, usually by graduates of France's elite schools. The choice of a minority candidate was remote and not politically viable.

The prediction that terrorists surely would attempt to test the resolve of America's new president would require intelligence sharing that was lacking on the part of federal agencies in the past. In 1963, prior to President Kennedy's fatal trip to Dallas, the FBI failed to notify the Secret Service about Lee Harvey Oswald and his ties to the Soviet Union. In 2001, the lack of coordinated data from the FBI, CIA, and National Security Agency regarding terrorists from the Middle East taking flying lessons in America enabled the disaster of September 11. Ironically, Ramzi bin al-Shibh, the Al Qaeda organizer of the airplane hijackings, noted that if the arrest of one of their men, Zacarias Moussaoui, on immigration charges in August had been known to the planners, the September attacks might have been cancelled. Perhaps war could have been avoided. On May 4, 2006, the day of his sentence to life in prison, rather than the death penalty, Moussaoui's last taunt in the courtroom was, "America you lost, you lost! . . . I won!"

Based on incomplete information, America went to war twice. The Tonkin Gulf incident in 1964, when enemy torpedoes were reported to have attacked two U.S. destroyers, came under review in 2001. The National Security Agency confirmed that 90 percent of the facts had been omitted from documents intended for Washington policy makers, who used them to authorize military action in Vietnam. In Iraq, the National Intelligence Estimate claimed that there were weapons of mass destruction, the spur to go to war. When none were found by United Nations inspectors, the rationale became to bring democracy to Iraqis suffering under the tyranny of Saddam Hussein. It reminded us of C. L. Sulzberger's words in the *International Herald Tribune*, February 1968, "Democracy is for those with a tradition of self-government, not for those accustomed to imposed authority." A presidential hopeful from Minnesota, Senator Eugene McCarthy, warned Americans that when society accepts injustice, corruption spreads.

The dehumanizing effect of war was clear. In 1968, in the village of My Lai, a U.S. infantry company massacred three hundred Vietnamese civilians, including women and children. In Iraq, it began in 2003 with the Abu Ghraib prison scandal, when American reservists humiliated and abused local prisoners. This was followed by the Haditha incident in 2005, involving five marines charged with killing twenty-four noncombatant civilians of all ages. Military investigators cited insufficient information for convicting the accused, an example of what aptly has been called the "fog of war." The Iraq and Afghanistan Wars were considered scandalous for "brutally sacrificing the psychological well-being" of our troops, assigned to long and repeated tours of duty. One of President Obama's first orders was to close Guantánamo, where abusive treatment of the detainees undermined American values.

General William Westmoreland, as commander of American forces in Vietnam, was sure that the war could have been won if only he had been given more troops. In 2007, President Bush first called for a "surge" of twenty thousand troops to support those already in Iraq. While deemed a success, the U.S. death toll exceeded four thousand, with tens of thousands more permanently disabled. America's war costs were $3 billion per week.

The latest request for additional troops came from the top U.S. general in Afghanistan in 2009. Whether to increase the military is the decision of the president as commander-in-chief, usually based on an actual threat to America, the long-term consequences globally and at home, and the political stability of a foreign country.

Living in Europe in the sixties, the Vietnam War seemed far away. Back in America, the news of each battle and casualty in Iraq and now in Afghanistan was a daily sorrow.

We often remember our years in Europe. By chance, the D'Gerolamo family who lived downstairs from us in the Neuilly apartment building was only an hour's drive away when we returned to America. Joan now is Dame Joan, having received the Papal Cross in 1992 by authority of Pope John Paul II for her seventeen years as the first administrator of the Saint John Vianney Residence for Retired Priests in Rutherford, New Jersey. In her inimitable way, Joan referred to the priests' residence as "a home for unwed fathers." She generously loaned me her saved copies of *Paris Match* for my research.

The value of life abroad was not lost on our own children. They both remember friends with whom they spoke another language, played, and celebrated birthdays. In the midst of a foreign culture, they became happy and outgoing. The discipline of French schooling at the Cours Montaigne – homework in the first grade and writing cursive script at age five – did no damage to Steven's psyche, even though cursive often is taught in American schools in the third grade based on educators who claim that children's motor skills develop later. Debby, who created stories and looked at her picture books in her room after mornings at the *jardin d'enfants*, applied her focus to a journalism career after college. She is a world traveler and eager to learn. We made a mistake by not continuing to speak French to them in America. English was the language of their new schoolmates – French just faded away. Andrew, born in France but raised in America, is a free spirit, interested in history and how events happen as they do. French was the language of choice for all three in high school, given the possibility that someday they might spend time overseas or with their cousins in Belgium (who all speak English).

The French storybooks, school notebooks, drawings, and records now are stored in the armoire, Europe's answer to inadequate closet space, which we shipped back when we moved home. On occasional visits, our grandchildren enjoy listening to the old 45 rpm records, even if they do not understand the words. Some of the songs are about dancing on the bridge of Avignon; calling the glazier to repair a broken window; Mère Michel who lost her cat; or Meunier, the miller, whose windmill spun too fast when he fell asleep – so different they are from Mary's little lamb, Jack and Jill, or the itsy bitsy spider.

Our story of two continents does not end. Many of the events that occurred during the sixties either have been, or are yet to be, resolved. The insights we gained of our country and Europe, the value of the friendships we formed with compatriots and people from other lands, now can be told by our children to theirs. They surely need remembering.

ACKNOWLEDGMENTS

With her usual efficiency, Jeanne-Françoise Roche in Paris expedited the securing of pictures and text permissions to complete this project.

My gratitude to those with special permissions and copyrights:

FOR PUBLISHERS: For their courtesy in confirming fair use of text quotes from their publications in America, Switzerland, and France, I should like to thank all of those listed in the Picture Credits and Bibliography-Source Lists.

FOR AUTHORS: Dominique Schnapper in Paris for Raymond Aron; the Borchardt Literary Agency for the French publishers of the works of Charles de Gaulle and Jean-Jacques Servan-Schreiber; the Estate of Eugene V. Epstein in Zurich; and Julia E. Murray in Los Angeles for Janet Flanner.

FOR CARTOONISTS AND PHOTOGRAPHS: The Margo Feiden Galleries in New York City for Al Hirschfeld; Jonathan M. Gordon in Los Angeles for the Estate of Bill Mauldin; Madame Martine Laplaine Méric in Louveciennes, France, for J. Lap (Jacques Laplaine); Solo Syndication in London for Vicky (Victor Weisz), and Moïse Taieb in Neuilly-sur-Seine for the synagogue photograph. *Le Canard Enchâiné* in Paris generously allowed photographing from its satirical newspaper, permitted use of the Escaro cartoon, and provided copyright sources for other artists whose work appeared in its pages.

FOR QUOTES IN FOREIGN EDITIONS DURING THE 1960s: from *U.S. News and World Report* in Washington D.C.; and from the *New York Times* in New York for the *International Herald Tribune* and the *New York Times*. Permissions from the current *New York Times* are from Pars Intl., also in New York.

I am indebted to Frances Malino, the Sophie Moses Robinson Professor of Jewish Studies at Wellesley College for her insights on Chapter 6b, "The Jews of France." Various readers were more than helpful in their comments and on the book's value for those who were too young to remember the Vietnam War.

And, always, to my husband for those exciting years in Europe during the sixties that we remember today.

BIBLIOGRAPHY AND SOURCES CITED

The following books provided useful backgrounds both to the events of the 1960s and to historic information where necessary in each chapter, and also to their current comparisons in the Epilogue. These are followed by Sources of quotes, paraphrases, and general information, either from these books or from specific newspapers, magazines, television programs, and the Internet. Some books are repeated for ease of reference. In each Source, dates are followed by page numbers. The letter *q* applies to the person quoted. *US News and World Report* is cited as *US News*. The *International Herald Tribune* and *New York Times* from the sixties, cited as *IHT* and *NYT*, are from the European editions. The current *New York Times*, published in America, is from the Late Edition.

Preface

BECKER, CARL. *Everyman His Own Historian*. Washington, D.C.: American Historical Association, 1931.

CARTIER-BRESSON, HENRI. *France*. Text by François Nourissier. New York: Viking Press, 1971.

COLOMBIANI, JEAN-MARIE, and WALTER WELLS. *Dangerous de-Liaisons: What's Really Behind the War Between France and the U.S.* Ed. Luc Jacob-Duvernet. Trans. Sarah Alexander. Hoboken, N.J.: Melville House, 2004.

COSTIGLIOLA, FRANK. *France and the United States: The Cold Alliance Since World War II.* New York: Twayne Publishers, 1992.

DRUTMAN, IRVING, ed. *Janet Flanner's World: Uncollected Writings, 1932-1975.* New York: Harcourt Brace Jovanovich, 1979.

FLANNER, JANET. *Paris Journal, 1964-1971*. Vol. 2. Ed. William Shawn. New York: Harcourt Brace Jovanovich, 1971. © Julia E. Murray.

GRAMONT, SANCHE DE. *The French: Portrait of a People*. New York: Putnam's Sons, 1969.

HIGHET, GILBERT, *The Anatomy of Satire*. Princeton: Princeton Univ. Press, 1962.

HITCHCOCK, WILLIAM. *The Struggle for Europe: The Turbulent History of a Divided Continent, 1945-2002*. New York: Doubleday, 2002.

KAGAN, ROBERT. *Of Paradise and Power*, New York: Knopf, 2003.

KUISEL, RICHARD. *Seducing the French: The Dilemma of Americanization*. Berkeley: Univ. of California Press, 1993.

MANDELBAUM, MICHAEL. *The Ideas That Conquered the World*. New York: Public Affairs, 2002.

NIXON, RICHARD M. *The Memoirs of Richard Nixon*. New York: Grosset & Dunlap, 1978.

PEYREFITTE, ALAIN. *The Trouble with France*. Trans. William R. Byron. New York: Knopf, 1981.

PRESS, CHARLES. *The Political Cartoon*. East Brunswick, N.J.: Associated University Presses, 1981.

REVEL, JEAN-FRANÇOIS. *Anti-Americanism*. Trans. Diarmid Cammell. San Francisco: Encounter Books, 2003.

WRIGHT, GORDON. *France in Modern Times*. 3rd ed. New York: W.W. Norton, 1981.

Preface Sources

p.13. memory is a guide to the present. . . . : Becker, 234, 237.

14. If America was threatened, France would be its ally: Kuisel, 144.

14. Vietnam War "leading a great nation to lay waste a small one":
      IHT, 2 January 1967, 1. q. de Gaulle.

14. United States, a giant stumbling around with a bag over its head . . . :
      Sanche de Gramont, *IHT*, 1967, n.d.

14. America "makes war well and peace poorly": Flanner, 2:199, 1 November 1967.
      q. André Malraux to India's Nehru.

14. De Gaulle: found the French to be ungovernable. . . . : Peyrefitte, 51.

Chapter 1. Zurich

AMERICAN WOMEN'S CLUB OF ZURICH, *Living in Zurich*. Zurich: AWCZ, 2001.

EPSTEIN, EUGENE V. *Take Me to Your Chalet*. Berne: Benteli, 1982. ©Estate of
      Eugene V. Epstein, Zurich.

_____. *Malice in Wonderland*. Berne: Benteli, 1985. ©ibid.

_____. *A Pain in the Alps*. Berne: Benteli, 1990. ©ibid.

_____. *Once Upon an Alp*, rev. ed. Basel: ©Bergli Books, 2002.

HÄSLER, ALFRED A. *The Lifeboat is Full: Switzerland and the Refugees,1933-1945*.
      Trans. Charles Lam Markmann. New York: Funk & Wagnalls, 1969.

MEDHURST, MARTIN J., ed. *Eisenhower's War of Words: Rhetoric and Leadership*.
      East Lansing, Mich.: Michigan State Univ., 1994 .

VINCENT, ISABEL. *Hitler's Silent Partners: Swiss Banks, Nazi Gold, and the Pursuit of
      Justice*. New York: William Morrow, 1997.

WAGNER, MEIR. *The Righteous of Switzerland: Heroes of the Holocaust*.
      Hoboken, N.J.: Ktav Publishing House, 2001.

ZIEGLER, JEAN. *The Swiss, the Gold, and the Dead: How Swiss Bankers Helped Finance
      the Nazi War Machine*. Trans. John Brownjohn. New York: Harcourt Brace, 1998.

Chapter 1. Sources

p.19. "Europe's Largest Skating Rink": *Weekly Tribune*, 8 February 1963, 1.

20. Swiss and Scandinavians wait "with a stop watch":
      "What U.S. Companies are Doing Abroad", *US News*, 9 March 1964, 86.

20. "gnomes of Zurich": Internet, "Gnomes of Zurich".

p. 22. 1962, "more peaceful than at any time in nearly thirty years":
      "Is the Danger Fading?", *US News*, 7 January 1963, 26.

23. "Americans take setbacks too seriously. . . .": "Why anti-Americanism?",
      US News, 30 March 1964, 61.

23. "Let them come to Berlin": "Europe After Kennedy", *US News*,
      8 July 1963, 35. q. Pres. Kennedy.

24. The Germans would "pay lip service . . .": "After the Kennedy Trip",
      US News, 15 July 1963, 35.

24. "What were we doing here anyway?": "From Vietnam", *US News*,
      5 August 1963, 46.

24. the "falling domino theory": Medhurst, 3.

24. "McNamara's War": Samantha Power, "War and Never Having to Say You're Sorry",
      NYT 12 December 2003, 1.

25. "With America's lack of staying power . . .": "Washington Whispers",
      US News, 21 January 1963, 28. q. Ho Chi Minh.

     25. "It seems inane. . . .": Epstein, 1985, 53.

25. "Don't you understand a Swiss joke . . .?": Epstein, 1982, 136.

25. "What gives you foreigners the right to criticize us. . . . Well?!":
      Epstein, 1990, 88-89.

27. "a cannon to shoot down a sparrow": *Newsweek*, 10 February 1964, 66,
      Business and Finance.

30. "We had a choice between security and politics. . . .": "Warren Commission Findings",
      US News, 6 July 1964, 44.

31. In praise of Kennedy: *NYT,* 26 November 1963, Letters to the Editor.

31. " Harvard is out . . .": *US News*, 9 December 1963, 6, Front Page of the Week.

31. "he gets results": "Lyndon Johnson's First Six Months", *US News*, 18 May 1964, 54.

31. Johnson, determined to "reason together": *US News*, 16 November 1964, 37.

32. Goldwater, "a sort of Rip van Winkle . . .": *US News*, 15 June 1964, 71, Worldgram.
      q. *The Guardian* (London).

32. "Extremism in the defense of liberty . . .": "Goldwater's Opening Gun", *US News*,
      27 July 1964, 96. q, Barry Goldwater.

32. "We cannot act rashly. . . .": "LBJ's Campaign Opener", *US News*, 7 September 1964, 67.

34. Grüezi, "the most important word . . .": Epstein, 2002, 44.

37. Paul Grüninger arrested for falsifying documents: Vincent, 124.

124

Chapter 2. Neuilly-sur-Seine

FLAGEOLLET, PIERRE. *Vie et Histoire de Neuilly-sur-Seine*. Paris: Editions Hervas, 1997.

MAURIAC, CLAUDE. *The Other de Gaulle: Diaries 1944-1945*. Trans. Noura Budberg and Gordon Latta. New York: John Day, an Intext Publisher, 1974.

NOURISSIER, FRANÇOIS. *The French*. Trans. Adrienne Foulke. New York: Knopf. 1968.

SAINT-EXUPÉRY, ANTOINE de. *Le Petit Prince*. Paris: Gallimard, 1943.

Chapter 2. Sources

p.41. "Neuilly! Charming sojourn . . .": Flageollet, 73. q. Alfred de Musset.

42. "But eyes are blind. . . .": Saint-Exupéry, 87.

42. "It is the hour to do good": Flageollet, 56. q. Neuilly clock inscription.

43. "rather better than what I would have liked": Mauriac, 43. q. Mme. De Gaulle.

45. World War I, "a hemorrhage that bled France white": Nourissier, 242.

45. "twelve million beautiful babies . . .": Internet, "Women in postwar France".
     q. De Gaulle.

Chapter 3. Charles de Gaulle

ADLER, BILL, ed. *The Churchill Wit*. New York: Coward McCann, 1965.

ARON, RAYMOND. *France, Steadfast and Changing: The Fourth to the Fifth Republic*. Cambridge: Harvard Univ. Press, 1960.

CHURCHILL, WINSTON S. *Blood, Sweat, and Tears*. New York: G.P.Putnam's Sons. 1941.

_____. Great Destiny. New York: G.P. Putnam's Sons, 1965.

COLLINS, LARRY, and DOMINIQUE LAPIERRE. *Is Paris Burning?* New York: Simon & Schuster, 1965.

COOK, DON. *Charles De Gaulle, a Biography*. New York: G.P. Putnam's Sons, 1983.

DUROSELLE, JEAN-BAPTISTE. *France and the United States: From the Beginnings to the Present*. Trans. Derek Coltman. Chicago: Univ. of Chicago Press. 1978.

EBAN, ABBA. *Autobiography*. New York: Random House, 1977.

_____. Heritage: *Civilization and the Jews*. New York: Summit Books, 1984.

FERRELL, ROBERT H., ed. *The Eisenhower Diaries*. New York: W.W. Norton, 1981.

FLANNER, JANET. *Paris Journal, 1964-1971*. Vol.2. Ed. William Shawn. New York: Harcourt Brace Jovanovich, 1971. ©Julia E. Murray.

GAULLE, CHARLES de. *War Memoirs: Unity, 1942-1944*. Trans. Richard Howard. © 1959 Charles de Gaulle. Originally appeared in French as *L'Unité*. ©1956 by Librairie Plon. Reprinted by permission of Georges Borchardt, Inc., for Librairie Plon.

GILDEA, ROBERT. *Marianne in Chains: Daily Life in the Heart of France During the German Occupation*. New York: Henry Holt, 2002.

GORDON, PHILIP H. *A Certain Idea of France: French Security Policy and the Gaullist Legacy*. Princeton, N.J.: Princeton Univ. Press, 1993.

HESS, JOHN L. *The Case for De Gaulle: An American Viewpoint*. New York: William Morrow, 1968.

HOFFMANN, STANLEY. *Decline or Renewal? France Since the 1930s*. New York: Viking Press, 1974.

LACOUTURE, JEAN. *De Gaulle: The Rebel, 1890-1944*. Trans. Alan Sheridan. New York: W.W. Norton, 1990.

_____. *De Gaulle: The Ruler, 1945-1970*. Trans. Alan Sheridan. New York: W.W. Norton, 1991.

LEDWIDGE, BERNARD. *De Gaulle*. New York: St. Martin's Press, 1982.

MAURIAC, CLAUDE. *The Other De Gaulle: Diaries 1944-1945*. Trans. ©1973 Angus & Robertson. New York: John Day Co. (Intext Publisher), 1974.

MEDHURST, MARTIN J., ed. *Eisenhower's War of Words: Rhetoric and Leadership*. East Lansing, Mich: Michigan State Univ., 1994.

SAINT-SIMON, DUC de (Louis de Rouvroy). *Memoirs of the Duc de Saint Simon on the Reign of Louis XIV*. Added author, Bayle St. John. Vol.2 (1710-1715), Vol.3 (1715-1723). London: G. Allen & Unwin, 1926.

SEDILLOT, RENÉ. *A Bird's Eye View of French History*. London: George Harrap, 1952.

SUFFERT, GEORGES. *Charles De Gaulle,1890-1970*. Paris: Les Editions du Groupe Express, 1970.

THOMPSON, ROBERT SMITH. *Pledge to Destiny: Charles De Gaulle and the Rise of the Free French*. New York: McGraw-Hill, 1974.

TUCHMAN, BARBARA. *March of Folly*. New York: Ballantine Books, 1984.

WILLIAMS, CHARLES. *The Last Great Frenchman: A Life of General de Gaulle*. New York: John Wiley & Sons, 1993.

Chapter 3. Sources

p.48. (Opening quote). "France! It is the country I serve. . . .": Mauriac, 295.
q. De Gaulle, 14 May 1948.

49. *"la gloire de la France"*: Hess, 84. q. De Gaulle.

49. "from the Atlantic to the Urals": Ledwidge, 276. q. De Gaulle.

49. Roosevelt's "Anglo-Saxon tendency to dominate": Ledwidge, 143, fn.19.
q. De Gaulle, in *L'Unité*, 79-81.

p. 49. England's "ruthless love of power": Thompson, 179. q. De Gaulle.

49. "We all have our crosses to bear. . . .": Adler, 65. q. Churchill.

49. De Gaulle's *force de frappe":* Ledwidge, 268.

50. "I could defy General Eisenhower. . . .": De Gaulle, 241.

50. "If I had not been there . . .": Mauriac, 299. q. De Gaulle, Aug. 5, 1948.

50. "an instrument of destiny . . .": Ledwidge,181, fn.17. q. De Gaulle in *L'Unité*, 311 ff.

50. "Messieurs, one step behind me.": Collins and Lapierre, 334.

50. "I'm afraid we shall never forgive him for it": Hess, 104.

51. "Charlie is my darling": Flanner, 2:176.

52. "will never free us of the debt we owe . . .": Flanner, 2:178, 5 April 1967.
       q. André François-Poncet, from "Amica America", *Le Figaro* (Paris), 23 March 1967,1.

52. "He was no more anti-American . . .": Ledwidge, 381.

52. "Monsieur le Ministre . . .": Nourissier, 243. q. De Gaulle.

52. "The Joint Chiefs of Staff do not believe . . .": Art Buchwald, "Handling De Galle",
       IHT 4 Jan. 1968, 12.

52. "domino theory": Tuchman, 262. q. Pres. Dwight Eisenhower, 7 April 1954,
       press conference.

54. "When de Gaulle hears this . . . It was a cruel plot. . .: Buchwald, op.cit.

55. "me or chaos": Seymour Freidin, "De Gaulle and Unity", *IHT*, 8 November 1967, 4,
       Editorial.

55. "De Gaulle doesn't exist. . . .": Henri de Turenne, "Grand Subject", *NYT* Magazine,
       12 September 1965, 114. q. Jean Cau, secretary to Jean-Paul Sartre.

55. "Long live free Quebec": Duroselle, 234. q. De Gaulle.

55. "All Canadians are free. . . .": *IHT*, 29-30 July 1967, 1. q. Lester Pearson.

55. "one of those oratorical escalations . . .": Ronald Koven, "De Gaulle 'Free Quebec'
       Cry Stirs Storm in French Press", IHT, 26 July 1967, 1. q. *Le Monde* (Paris).

55. Moscow would "terrorize Western Europe": James Reston, "NATO and the East
       European Crisis", *IHT*, 10-21 July 1968.

55. "the great Russian people": Ledwidge, 359, fn.2. q. De Gaulle, 9 September 1968,
       in *Discours et Messages*, 5:334-5.

56. "People get the history they deserve. . . .", "There are moments . . .", a defeatist attitude was
       "worse than stupidity . . .": Ledwidge, 29, fn. 6. q. De Gaulle, in J-R. Tournoux,
       La Tragédie du Général (Annexe), 514.

Chapter 4. The French

BIRNBAUM, PIERRE. *The Idea of France*. Trans. M.B. DeBevoise. New York: Hill & Wang, 1998.

CAESAR, JULIUS. *The Battle for Gaul*. Trans. Anne and Peter Wiseman. Boston:
David R. Godine, 1980.

ETIEMBLE, RENÉ. *Parlez-vous franglais*. Paris: ©Editions Gallimard, 1991.

FLANNER, JANET. *Paris Journal, 1965-1971*. Vol. 2. Ed. William Shawn. New York:
Harcourt Brace Jovanovich, 1971. ©Julia E. Murray.

KAGAN, ROBERT. *Of Paradise and Power*. New York: Knopf, 2003.

KARNOW, STANLEY, *Vietnam, a History*. Viking Press, 1983.

KUISEL, RICHARD F. *Seducing the French: The Dilemma of Americanization*.
Berkeley: Univ. of California Press, 1993.

LEE, JENNIFER. *Paris in Mind: Three Centuries of Americans Writing About Paris*.
New York: Vintage Books, 2003.

NADEAU, JEAN-BENOIT, and JULIE BARLOW. *Sixty Million Frenchmen Can't Be Wrong:
Why We Love France, but Not the French*. Naperville, Ill: Sourcebooks, 2003.

NOURISSIER, FRANÇOIS. *The French*. Trans. Adrienne Foulke. New York: Knopf, 1968.

PEYREFITTE, ALAIN. *The Trouble with France*. Trans. William R. Byron. New York: Knopf, 1981.

REDMAN, BEN RAY, ed. *The Portable Voltaire*. New York: Viking Penguin, 1977.

SCHOENBRUN, DAVID. *As France Goes*. New York: Harper & Bros., 1957.

SIEGFRIED, ANDRÉ. "The French Mind." In *Readings in Exposition*. Ed. Harry B. Reed and
Julia Norton McCorkle, 273-285. New York: Harcourt, Brace, 1942.

THACKER, CHRISTOPHER. *Voltaire*. Profiles in Literature Series. Ed. B.C. Southam. New York:
Humanities Press, 1971.

WHITE, EDMUND. *The Flaneur: A Stroll Through the Paradoxes of Paris*. New York: Bloomsbury, 2001.

WYLIE, LAURENCE. *Village in the Vaucluse*. Cambridge: Harvard Univ. Press,
©1957, 1964, 1974, by the President and Fellows of Harvard College.

Chapter 4. Sources

p.59. "At the current rate of corruption . . . gibberish that I call *franglais*":
Thomas R. Bransten, "Paris Professor Fights Invasion of Language by Anglicisms",
IHT, 16 October 1962, 10.

59. 18th century, "drawing room", "roast beef", "toast": Etiemble, 267.

59. 19th century, "lunch", "touring", "boarding house", "high life": Etiemble, 269.

59. 20th century military terms, "jeep", "half-track", "commando": Etiemble 270.

59. publicity terms, "thrilling", "ultramodern", "streamlined": Etiemble 289.

p.60. English words in *Le Petit Larousse*: "quick-freezing": Etiemble, 357, 385.
    "discount", "battle dress": Etiemble, 409.

60. Suggestions to combat franglais, to children: Etiemble, 394.

60. to radio and television announcers: Etiemble, 391.

60. to merchants with publicity posters: Etiemble, 392.

60. French as in the time of Mme. de Sévigné: Etiemble. 415. q. Bransten, op.cit.

60. The French resembled ill-tempered Italians: Peyrefitte, 265. q. Jean Cocteau.

60-61. "In Paris you can live for twenty years in an apartment. . . ., Foreigners who find
    us so little hospitable . . .": Nourissier, 215, 216-17.

62. "Being appreciated . . .": Jean-Benoit Nadeau, "Learning to Love the French",
    interview by Julie Salamon. *NYT*,14 July 2003. E.1,4.

62. "every man for himself" attitude: Peyrefitte, 218. q. De Gaulle.

62. "How can France be governed . . .?", "rally around their national pride", "dissolve in
    mediocrity": Peyrefitte, 51-52. q. De Gaulle.

63. "The necessity of saying something . . .": Letters on the English or *Lettres
    Philosophiques*, XXIV, On the Royal Society and Other Academies. q. Voltaire.

66. "How can a child avoid feeling. . . .?", he "manipulates the system . . .": Wylie, 311.

66. "constant competition . . . ": Schoenbrun, 206.

68. *Humanae Vitae*: Internet, *Humanae Vitae*, On the Regulation of Birth, July 25,1968.

69. "the *congés payés*": Flanner 2:108, 3 August 1966.

69. staggered vacation time: Flanner 2:52, 28 June 1965.

69. "There isn't a cat in Paris": Flanner, 2:63, 10 August 1965.

Chapter 5. America: Vietnam and Civil Rights

CROZIER, MICHEL. *The Trouble With America: Why the System is Breaking Down.*
    Berkley: Univ. of California Press, 1984.

FURER, HOWARD B., ed. *Lyndon B. Johnson*. Dobbs Ferry, N.Y.: Oceana Publications, 1971.

GITLIN, TODD. The Sixties: Years of Hope, Days of Rage, rev.ed. New York: Bantam Books, 1993.

GETTLEMAN, MARVIN E., ed. *Vietnam: History, Documents, and Opinions on a Major World Crisis.*
    Greenwich, Conn.: Fawcett Publications, 1965.

HALBERSTAM, DAVID. "Crucial Point in Vietnam." In *Written into History: Pulitzer Prize
    Reporting of the Twentieth Century*. Ed. Anthony Lewis, 25-32. *NYT Books*, 2001.

JOHNSON, LYNDON BAINES. *The Vantage Point: Perspectives of the Presidency, 1963-1969.*

KALB, MARVIN, and ELIE ABEL. *Roots of Involvement: The United States in Asia, 1784-1971.* New York: W.W. Norton, 1971.

KARNOW, STANLEY. *Vietnam: A History.* New York: Viking Press, 1983.

LACOUTURE, JEAN. *De Gaulle, the Ruler,1945-1970.* Trans. Alan Sheridan. New York: W.W.Norton, 1991.

LEWIS, ANTHONY. *Struggle for Civil Rights, 1954-68.* New York: *NYT* Special Commemorative Section.

MARANISS, DAVID. *They Marched into Sunlight: War and Peace, Vietnam and America, October 1967.* New York: Simon & Schuster, 2003.

MEDURST, MARTIN. *Eisenhower's War of Words.* East Lansing, Mich.: Michigan State Univ., 1994.

NIXON, RICHARD M. *Memoirs of Richard Nixon.* New York: Grosset & Dunlap, 1978.

TUCHMAN, BARBARA W. *The March of Folly: From Troy to Vietnam.* New York: Knopf, 1984.

Chapter 5. Sources

p.73. President Kennedy escalated advisers without Congress authorization: Tuchman, 299.

73."I made it a rule for myself . . .": Johnson, 23.

74. unfamiliar jungle warfare . . . , imposing democracy: C.L. Sulzberger, "Strategy of Error: I", *IHT,* 28 February 1968,1.

74. "The Vietnamese people have never done any harm. . . .": The U.S. must stop "barbaric methods of warfare . .", "all the people of the world . .": Johnson, 594, Appendix A, IX. q. Ho Chi Minh's Reply, 15 February 1967.

74. "U.S. Go Home" banner: Ronald Koven, "Flag Burning, Jeering Mobs Greet Visit by Vice President", *IHT*, 8-9 April 1967,1.

74. "No comment . . .": Don Cook, "De Gaulle-Humphrey Meeting is Cordial but Unproductive", *IHT,* 8-9 April 1967, 1. q. Humphrey.

75. "Violence is as American as cherry pie": *US News*, 7 August 1967, 8, March of the News. q. H. Rap Brown, news conference, Wash. D.C. July 27, '67.

76. "You can't trust anyone over thirty": "Crackdown Starts on Student Riots ", *US News*, 1 January 1968, 34.

76. "The time is past. . . .": Internet, "Catonsville Nine". q. Daniel Berrigan.

76. not "spanked enough as they grew up": " A Truman Plan for the South", *US News*, 30 September 1963, 15, People of the Week. q. Harry Truman at a testimonial dinner for Ohio senator Stephen Young.

77. "Power can lose its charm. . . .": Johnson, 433.

77. "Hey hey, LBJ . . .": Maraniss, 70.

77. "All that I could do I had done": Johnson, 437.

77. Johnson's move was courageous: Lacouture, 384. q. De Gaulle.

p.77. "the most far-reaching civil rights law . . .": E. W. Kenworthy, "President Signs
    Civil Rights Bill", *NYT*, 3 July 1964, 1.

78. civil rights legislation, the death of the Democratic Party in the South: Lewis, 2.

78. "the first president to lose a war": Nixon, 397.

78. Vietnam War, one of "mutual miscalculation": Nixon, 414.

78. Nixon's goal, "peace with honor": Transcript, Nixon's speech on Vietnam,
    NYT, 24 January 1973, 1, 16.

78. "Vietnam syndrome": Internet, Norman Solomon, "Beyond the 'Vietnam Syndrome'",
    14 September 2005.

 78. "Without allies and associates . . .": Medhurst, 113. q. Eisenhower.

Chapter 6a. 1967: Six-Day War

ARON, RAYMOND. *De Gaulle, Israel and the Jews*. Trans. John Sturrock. With a new
    introduction by Michael Curtis. New Brunswick, N.J.: Transaction Publishers, 2004.
    By permission of the publisher and Dominique Schnapper.

_____. *Memoirs: Fifty Years of Political Reflection*. Trans. George Holoch. New York:
    Holmes & Meier, 1990. By permission of the publisher and Dominique Schnapper.

EBAN, ABBA. *Autobiography*. New York: Random House, 1977.

GAULLE, CHARLES de. *Memoirs of Hope: Renewal and Endeavor, 1958-1962*.
    Trans. Terence Kilmartin, ©1971 by George Weidenfeld and Nicolson.
    Originally appeared in French as *Memoires d'Espoir: Le Renouveau, 1958-1962,
    L'Effort ,1962-* ©1970,1971, by Librairie Plon. Reprinted by permission of
    Georges Borchardt, Inc., for Librairie Plon.

LACOUTURE, JEAN. *De Gaulle: the Ruler, 1946-1970*. Trans. Alan Sheridan. New York:
    W.W. Norton, 1991.

MARSHALL, Brig. Gen. S.L.A., and Editors of American Heritage and United Press Intl.
    Swift Sword: The Historical Record of Israel's Victory, June 1967.
    New York: American Heritage Publishing Co., 1967.

OREN, MICHAEL B. *Six Days of War: June 1967 and the Making of the Modern Middle East*.
    New York: Oxford Univ. Press, 2002.

p.81. "an attempt to strangle a nation": Internet, Security Council Official Records.
    S/PV 1348, June 1967, Entry 175. q. Eban.

82. Israel, "our friend, our ally": Servan-Schreiber, "A Gaullist Looks at the Mideast Crisis" ,
    IHT, 2 June 1967, 4, Editorial. q. De Gaulle.

82. "Do not make war. Do not be the first to shoot": Eban, 341. q. De Gaulle.

82. "1967 was not 1957": Eban, 344. q. De Gaulle.

83. "France has . . . only interests": Aron 2004, 66.

83. "but not when the objective smells of petrol . . .": Aron 2004, 31.

83. "Israel did not follow my advice": Aron 1990, 350. q. De Gaulle.

83. "The Algerian crisis and the Suez affair . . .": De Gaulle, 264.

83. "Do not let your emotions . . .": Oren, 167. q. Andrei Gromyko to Katriel Katz,
    Israeli ambassador to Soviet Russia.

83. when in doubt strike: Marshall, 133.

83. a case of Israel's survival: Oren, 134.

84. "There is no difference between one Arab people and another. . . .": Oren, 137.
    q. King Hussein of Jordan.

84. "wipe Israel off the map . . .": Oren, 164. q. Abdul Rahman Aref of Iraq.

84. "U Thant's war": *US News*, 19 June 1967, 25.

84. "undercover guerrillas are being trained in sabotage. . . .": Pierre Macaigne,
    "La drole de paix" (The strange peace), part 2. *Le Figaro* (Paris),
    4 December 1968, 5.

85. "border incidents, acts of sabotage, and frantic agitation": Aron 2004, 15.
    q. De Gaulle to Walter Eytan, Israeli ambassador to France.

85. "an elite people, sure of themselves . . . ": Ledwidge, 332. q. De Gaulle.

85. "discrimination at the highest level": "De Gaulle and the Jews", *Newsweek*,
    11 December 1967, 47. q. Rabbi Jacob Kaplan, chief rabbi of France.

85. "to emphasize the character . . .": *Le Figaro* (Paris), 10 January 1968, 3.
    q. De Gaulle.

85. "the unpleasant smell of anti-Semitism": *Newsweek*, 11 December 1967, 47.
    q. *Le Monde* (Paris).

85. "to use the same language . . .": Aron 2004, 24.

85. "What would de Gaulle have offered Israel . . .?": Aron 1990, 350.

85. Ben-Gurion and de Gaulle letters: *Le Figaro* (Paris), 10 January 1968, 3.
    (Note: Ben-Gurion's letter, Dec. 6, '67; de Gaulle's reply, Dec. 30, '67)

86. "the only Western head of state . . .": Lacouture, 446. q. Nasser re de Gaulle.

Chapter 6b. Jews of France: A History

ADAMS, GEOFFREY. *The Huguenots and French Opinion, 1685-1787: the Enlightenment Debate on Toleration*. Waterloo, Ontario: Wilfrid Laurier Univ. Press, 1991.

ARON, RAYMOND. *De Gaulle, Israel and the Jews*. Trans. John Sturrock. With a new introduction by Michael Curtis. New Brunswick: Transaction Publishers, 2004. By permission of the publisher and Dominique Schnapper.

BEINART, HAIM. *The Expulsion of the Jews from Spain*. Trans. Jeffrey M. Green. Portland, Oregon: Littman Library of Jewish Civilization, 2002.

BENBASSA, ESTHER, *The Jews of France: A History from Antiquity to the Present*. Trans. M.B. DeBevoise. Princeton: Princeton Univ. Press, 1999.

BIRNBAUM, PIERRE, and IRA KATZNELSON, eds. *Paths of Emancipation: Jews, States, and Citizenship*. Princeton: Princeton Univ. Press, 1995.

COOK, DON. *Charles de Gaulle, A Biography*. New York: G.P. Putnam's Sons, 1983.

DREYFUS, ALFRED. *Five Years of My Life, 1894-1890*. New York: McClure, Phillips, 1901.

FOA, ANNA. *The Jews of Europe after the Black Death*. Trans. Andrea Grover. Berkeley: Univ. of California Press, 2000.

GILMAN, C. MALCOLM B. *The Huguenot Migration in Europe and America, Its Cause and Effect*. Red Bank, N.J.: Arlington Laboratory for Clinical and Historical Research, 1962.

HERTZBERG, ARTHUR. *The French Enlightenment and the Jews*. New York: Columbia Univ. Press, 1968.

HYMAN, PAULA. *The Jews of Modern France*. Berkeley and Los Angeles: Univ. of California Press, 1998.

KAMINS, TONI L. *Complete Jewish Guide to France*. New York: St. Martin's Griffin, 2001.

KEDOURIE, ELIE, ed. *The Jewish World: History and Culture of the Jewish People*. New York: Harry N. Abrams, 1979.

KOBLER, FRANZ. *Napoleon and the Jews*. New York: Schocken Books, 1976.

MALINO, FRANCES. *The Sephardic Jews of Bordeaux: Assimilation and Emancipation in Revolutionary and Napoleonic France*. University, Alabama: Univ. of Alabama Press, 1978.

MALINO, FRANCES, and BERNARD WASSERSTEIN, eds. *The Jews in Modern France*. Hanover, N.J.: University Press of New England for Brandeis Univ. Press, 1985.

ROTHSCHILD, GUY de. *The Whims of Fortune*. New York: Random House, 1985.

SOBOUL, ALBERT. *The French Revolution, 1787-1799: From the Storming of the Bastille to Napoleon*. Trans. Alan Forrest and Colin Jones. New York: Vintage Books, 1974.

SZAJKOWSKI, ZOSA. *Jews and the French Revolutions of 1789, 1830 and 1848*. New York: Ktav Publishing House, 1970.

TULARD, JEAN. *The French Revolution in Paris Seen through the Collections of the Carnavalet Museum*. Paris: Paris-Musées, 1989.

VOLTAIRE. *Candide, Zadig and Selected Stories*. Trans. with an Introduction by Donald M. Frame. Bloomington, Ind.: Indiana Univ. Press, 1961.

ZENOUDA, SYLVIE. *La Synagogue de Neuilly-Sur-Seine: 120 Ans d'Histoire d'une Communauté*. Paris: Y. Masson, 2000.

ZOLA, EMILE. *The Dreyfus Affair: J'accuse and Other Writings*. Ed. Alain Pagès. Trans. ©1996 Eleanor Levieux. New Haven: Yale Univ Press, 1996.

Chapter 6b. Sources

p.88. "a nation within a nation": Malino and Wasserstein, 292.

88. De Gaulle, "knowingly opened a new period in Jewish history. . . .": Aron, 25.

88. "Many Jews wept. . . .": Aron, 49.

88. "our friend, our ally": Jean-Jacques Servan-Schreiber, "A Gaullist Looks at the Mideast Crisis", *IHT*, 2 June 1967, 4. q. De Gaulle.

89. "faith in princes": Psalm 146:3.

89. "How does it come to pass that so great a king . . .?": Voltaire, 278.

90. (caption): "May his glory shine": Internet, International Napoleonic Society, 5, Prayer of the children of Israel.

91. "*J'accuse*"": Zola, 43.

91. Dreyfus trial, "one of the most iniquitous acts of this century": Zola, 52.

92. "Under the surface of the social privileges from which I'd benefited . .": Rothschild, 132.

92. "My only crime was to have been born a Jew": Dreyfus, 45.

93. *Vive la France! ":* Cook, 287. q. Pierre Laval.

93. "a great man ruined by ambition and age": Mauriac, 109. q. De Gaulle re Philippe Pétain.

93. Both men lacked "a sense of state": Mauriac, 130. q. De Gaulle.

94. "in return for their agreement to perform their civic duty": Hertzberg, 364.

Chapter 7. 1968: Days of May — Strikes and Riots

ARON, RAYMOND. *The Elusive Revolution: Anatomy of a Student Revolt*. Trans. Gordon Clough. New York: Praeger, 1969.

ALI, TARIQ, and SUSAN WATKINS. *1968: Marching in the Streets*. New York: Free Press, 1998.

BROWN, BERNARD. *Protest in Paris: Anatomy of a Revolt*. Morristown, N.J.: General Learning Press, 1974.

CAUTE, DAVID. *The Year of the Barricades: A Journey Through 1968*. New York: Harper & Row, 1988.

COOK, DON. *Charles de Gaulle: A Biography*. New York: G.P. Putnam's Sons, 1983.

FLANNER, JANET. *Paris Journal, 1964-1971*. Vol.2. Ed. William Shawn. New York: Harcourt Brace Jovanovich, 1971. © Julia E.Murray.

GALLANT, MAVIS. *Paris Notebooks: Essays and Reviews*. New York: Random House, 1986.

HESS, JOHN L. *The Case for De Gaulle: An American Viewpoint*. New York: William Morrow, 1968.

LACOUTURE, JEAN. *The Ruler,1945-1970*. Trans. Alan Sheridan. New York: W.W. Norton, 1991.

LEDWIDGE, BERNARD. *Charles de Galle*. New York: St. Martin's Press, 1982.

SERVAN-SCHREIBER, JEAN-JACQUES. *The American Challenge*. Trans. Ronald Steel. Originally appeared in French as *Le Défi Américain*. ©1967 by Editions Denoel. Reprinted by permission of Georges Borchardt, Inc., for Editions Denoel.

SUFFERT, GEORGE. *Charles de Gaulle, 1890-1970*. Paris: Edite-Union III, 1970.

WILLIAMS, CHARLES. *The Last Great Frenchman*. New York: John Wiley & Sons, 1993.

WRIGHT, GORDON. *France in Modern Times*. New York: W.W. Norton, 1995.

ZOLA, EMILE. *The Dreyfus Affair: 'J'accuse' And Other Writings*. Ed. Alain Pagès. Trans. ©1996 Eleanor Levieux. New Haven: Yale Univ. Press, 1996. Paris: CNRS, 1944.

Chapter 7. Sources

p. 96. student *enragés* of "vaguely Trotskyite persuasions": "Unrest in France", *NYT* , 19 May 1968, 1, Week in Review.

96. Nanterre University student population growth: Jean Maquet, "Quand la Jeunesse a Froid le Monde Entier Grelotte" (When Youth is Cold, the Whole World Shivers), *Paris Match*, 18 May 1968, 60-61. q. Prof. Gilles Ferry.

96. "jostling with them in the halls": "France at the Barricades", *Newsweek*, 27 May 1968, 42. q. Prof. Pierre Nordom, Institute of English Studies, Sorbonne.

97. exams called "sudden death": Lloyd Garrison, "French Students to the Streets", *NYT*, 12 May 1968, 1, Week in Review.

97. dropout rate after the first year . . . : Brown, 1.

97. overthrow of the "capitalist establishment": Lloyd Garrison, "Sorbonne Closed as Students Riot", *NYT*, 4 May 1968, 1.

97. "Paris might not have fallen. . . . : Flanner, 2:52-53, 16 May 1968.

98. "The chief of state should not be in the front lines. . . .": Cook, 402. q. De Gaulle.

98. "De Gaulle has only to turn his back. . . ., Play time is over!": Lacouture, 535. q. De Gaulle.

99. the situation was "incomprehensible": Wright, 443. q. De Gaulle.

99. "a terrible shock: "De la rue Gay-Lussac Va Partir La 'Terrible Secousse'" (From the rue Gay-Lussac the "Terrible Shock" Will Start), *Paris Match*, 22 June 1968, 56. q. De Gaulle.

99. force would be used: Wright, 443.

p. 99. "France for the French", "Cohn Bendit to Dachau": Ali and Watkins, 105.

    100. Gaullist cabinet ministers' interests . . . : "Vous avez compris?" (Did you understand?),
        Canard Enchâiné (Paris), 15 May 1968, 1.

    101. Days of May – a Retrospective: Zola, 29-30, 34-35.

    103. the referendum, "regionalization", "participation": Suffert, 364.

    103. "at whatever price": Lacouture, 539, q. De Gaulle to Pompidou.

    103. "A nation holding a monopoly of power . . . ": Servan-Schreiber, 102.

    103. "a strong, technologically united Europe . . .": Servan-Schreiber, 175.

    103. "to be masters in our own house": "One World: Dream That is Fading",
        US News, 14 October 1968, 63. q. De Gaulle.

    103. "legal strait jacket . . .": Servan-Schreiber, 254, fn.3, from Lawrence Wylie,
        In Search of France. Cambridge, Mass.: Harvard Univ. Press, 1963, 207-8.

    104. America, "Europe with a 15-year head start": Servan-Schreiber, 101.

    104. "This wager on man . . .": Servan-Schreiber, 253.

    105. "the analysis is sound . . .": Flanner, 2:222, 10 January 1968. q. De Gaulle re Servan-Schreiber's book.

    105. Gold, "does not change its nature": Hess, 126. q. De Gaulle.

    105. De Gaulle's "second *force de frappe*": Ledwidge, 343.

    105. "the worst possible absurdity": *US News*, 25 November 1968, 70, Business Around the World.

Chapter 8. 1969. Endings and Beginnings

ALEXANDRE, PHILIPPE. *The Duel: De Gaulle and Pompidou: A Candid Account of the
    Stormy Relationship Between France's Recent Presidents.* Trans. Elaine P. Halperin.
    Boston: Houghton Mifflin, 1972.

FLANNER, JANET. *Paris Journal, 1964-1971*. Vol.2. Ed. William Shawn. New York:
    Harcourt Brace Jovanovich, 1971. ©Julia E. Murray.

GAULLE, CHARLES de, *War Memoirs: Salvation, 1944-1946*. Trans. Richard Howard.
    ©1959. 1960 by Charles de Gaulle. Originally appeared in French as *Le Salut*. ©1959
    by Librairie Plon. Reprinted by permission of Georges Borchardt, Inc. for Librairie Plon.

GOSCINNY, RENÉ and ALBERT UDERZO. *Asterix the Gaul*. Trans. Anthea Bell, and Derek
    Hockridge. New York: William Morrow, 1970.

_____. *Asterix and the Roman Agent*. Trans. Anthea Bell, and Derek Hockridge.
    Leicester, England: Brockhampton Press, 1972.

_____. *Asterix at the Olympic Games*. 3d ed. Trans. Anthea Bell, and Derek Hockridge.
    Leicester, England: Brockhampton Press, 1973.

HEROLD, J. CHRISTOPHER. Horizon Book of *The Age of Napoleon*. New York:
    American Heritage,1963.

HOFFMANN, STANLEY. *Decline or Renewal? France Since the 1930s.* New York: Viking Press, 1974.

KINDLEBERGER, CHARLES. "Origins of United States Direct Investments in France." *Business History Review*, no.48 (Fall 1974): 381-413.

LACOUTURE, JEAN. *De Gaulle: The Ruler, 1945-1970.* Trans. Alan Sheridan. New York:. W.W. Norton, 1991.

LEDWIDGE, BERNARD. *De Gaulle.* New York: St. Martin's Press, 1982.

MAURIAC, CLAUDE. *The Other De Gaulle: Diaries 1944-1945.* Trans. Noura Budberg and Gordon Latta. New York: John Day, an Intext Publisher, 1974.

NIXON, RICHARD M. *Memoirs of Richard Nixon.* New York: Grosset & Dunlap, 1978.

NORA, PIERRE. "Americans and the French Intellectuals," *Daedalus 107* (Winter 1978): 325-337.

PFAFF, WILLIAM. "The French Exception." *New Yorker*, 13 January 1977, 66-75.

SINGER, BRUCE. *100 Years of the Paris Trib: From the Archives of the International Herald Tribune.* New York: Harry N. Abrams, 1987.

Chapter 8. Sources

p.108. "a day of warning": "A Day of Warning", *IHT*, 13 March 1968, 4, Editorial.

108. De Gaulle's "willingness to treat millions of his citizens with contempt . . .": "French Strike Falls Flat", *IHT*, 14 March 1969, 4, Editorial.

108. "de-Napoleonize France": Hoffmann, 249.

108. "Do you favor regionalization?", "Should the senate be transformed . . .?": Flanner 2:306, 9 April 1969.

108. Opponents were "fanatics of destruction . . .": Ronald Koven, "De Gaulle Tells French to Vanquish Malaise", *IHT*, 1 January 1969, 1. q. De Gaulle, New Year's Eve address.

109. referendum was "absurd": Lacouture, 573. q. Malraux.

109. (caption): "Everything failed me . . .!": Herold, 356. q. Napoleon at Battle of Waterloo (according to Comte Emmanuel Las Cases).

110. "when they wake up . . .": Lacouture, 576. q. De Gaulle.

110. "melancholy woods and meadows, old mountains . . ." : De Gaulle, 328.

110. "The general is happy now": Alexandre, 6. q. Mme. De Gaulle.

110. De Gaulle, "one who really believes himself . . .": Mauriac, 193.

110. "This is my home. . . . always watching . . . for the gleam of hope": De Gaulle, 328-30.

111. Tintin, "my only international rival": Lacouture, 584. De Gaulle.

111 "Le Jour de Merci Donnant": Art Buchwald, *IHT*, 25 November 1965.

112. Getafix, Obelix, Vitalstatistix and Cacafonix, Crismus Bonus, Marcus Ginantonicus: Goscinny and Uderzo, 1970, 4ff, 6ff, 21.

112. Magnumopus: Goscinny and Uderzo, 1972, 24ff.

p. 112. Gluteus Maximus: Goscinny and Uderzo, 1973, 5ff.

112. "In 88 hours and 50 minutes . . .": Jean Cau, "Ce sont les Conquérants d'une nouvelle Planète" (These are the Conquerors of a New Planet), *Paris Match*, 26 July 1969, 21-27.

112. "This is a new ocean . . .": *Time Magazine*, 2 March 1962, 11. q. President Kennedy.

112. The earth, "big and bright and beautiful": Singer, 187. Reprint of Al Rossiter Jr., "Man on moon", *IHT*, 21 July 1969, 1. q. Neil Armstrong.

113. "Poor Pompidou": Ledwidge, 375.

113. " . . . I can't even go for a short walk about Paris!": Alexandre, 1.

113. "France is a widow": Flanner, 2:410. q. Pompidou. 11 November 1970.

Epilogue: Then and Now

ANDELMAN, DAVID A. *A Shattered Peace*. Hoboken, N.J.: John Wiley & Sons, 2008.

ARON, RAYMOND, *De Gaulle, Israel and the Jews*. Trans. John Sturrock. With a new Introduction by Michael Curtis. New Brunswick, N.J.: Transaction Publishers, 2004. By permission of the publisher and Dominique Schnapper.

DAALDER, IVO H., and James M. Lindsay. *America Unbound: The Bush Revolution in Foreign Policy*. Washington D.C.: Brookings Institution, 2003.

GAULLE, CHARLES de. *War Memoirs. Hope: Renewal and Endeavor, 1958-1962*. Trans. Terence Kilmartin. New York: Simon & Schuster, 1971. Originally appeared in French as *Memoires d'Espoir: Le Renouveau 1958-1962, L'Effort* 1962-. ©1970-71 by Librairie Plon. Reprinted by permission of Georges Borchardt, Inc., for Librairie Plon.

GOLDSTEIN, GORDON M. *Lessons in Disaster: McGeorge Bundy and the Path to War in Vietnam,* New York: Times Books/Henry Holt, 2008.

HÄSLER, ALFRED, *The Lifeboat is Full*. Trans. Alfred Lam Markmann. New York: Funk & Wagnalls, 1969.

KIMBALL, ROGER. *The Long March: How the Cultural Revolution of the 1960s Changed America*. San Francisco: Encounter Books, 2000.

LEWIS, ANTHONY. *Struggle for Civil Rights 1954-1968*. New York: *NYT* Special Commemorative Section.

SARKOZY, NICOLAS. *Testimony: France in the Twenty-first Century*. Trans. © 2007 Philip Gordon. New York: Pantheon Books, 2007.

SERVAN-SCHREIBER, JEAN-JACQUES. *The American Challenge*. Trans. Ronald Steel. Originally appeared in French as *Le Défi Américain*. ©1967 by Editions Denoel. Reprinted by permission of Georges Borchardt, Inc., for Editions Denoel.

WEINER, TIM. *Legacy of Ashes: The History of the CIA*. New York: Doubleday, 2007.

WOODWARD, BOB. *Plan of Attack*. New York: Simon & Schuster, 2004.

Epilogue Sources

p. 116. Paul Grüninger vindicated: Häsler, clipping on inside book cover, from a Geneva correspondent. (See Ch.I:37)

116. Holocaust claims were a conspiracy . . .: Jane Kramer, "Manna from Hell", *New Yorker*, 28 April - 5 May 1997, 89. q. Robert Holzach.

116. No nation can prevail militarily . . .: Elaine Sciolino, "An Admirer of America Sets a New Course for France", *NYT*, 8 May 2007, 8. q. Sarkozy.

116. "frantic agitation". (See p.132:85, Aron 2004. 15)

116. Six-Day war, a "wasted victory": *The Economist,* May 26, 2007, 13.

117. America, the sole superpower: Servan-Schreiber, 102. (See Ch. VII:103)

117. "Much of what is good around us . . .": Garry Wills, "The 60s, Tornado of Wrath", *Newsweek,* 3 January 1994, 41.

117. . . . the Democrats lost the South: Lewis, 2 .(See Ch. V:78)

118. "Democracy is for those with a tradition of self-government . . .": C.L. Sulzberger, "The Strategy of Error: I, *IHT* , 28 February 1968, (See Ch. V:74)

118. "when society accepts injustice . . ." : Roger Kahn, "The Quiet Man", *NYT* 19 December 2005, 33. q. Senator Eugene McCarthy.

118. "America, you lost, you lost! . . . I won.": Neil A. Lewis, "Moussaoui Given Life Term by Jury Over Link to 9/11", *NYT* , 4 May 2006, I. q. Zacarias Moussaoui.

118. "fog of war": Eugenia C. Kiesling, Military Review (September-October 2001), 85.

118. Iraq and Afghanistan Wars "brutally sacrificing the psychological well-being . . .", Bob Herbert, "Wars Psychic Toll," *NYT*, 19 May 2004, 24.

118. America's war costs: "Back from Iraq, Again Facing Fire", *NYT*, 8 April 2008, 27.

PICTURE CREDITS

As each subject varies, credits are listed by chapter and page in the following order as applicable: cartoonist, subject, copyright source (supplemented in the abbreviations below), photo source, publication, date. Some credits also are noted with the photo in the chapters as requested.

AF	Ada Feyerick
ACIP	Association Consistoriale Israélite de Paris (Neuilly)
ARS/ADAGP	Representing Roland Moisan and Jean Effel: © 2008 Artists Rights Society, NYC; Sociétés des Auteurs dans les Arts Graphiques et plastique (ADAGP), Paris
BnF	Bibliothèque nationale de France
CE	Courtesy of Canard Enchâiné, Paris
Escaro	By permission of Escaro, Canard Enchâiné
HB	1967 Herblock cartoon. © by the Herb Block Foundation, Washington, D.C.
IHT	International Herald Tribune, Paris
LC	Courtesy of Library of Congress, Prints and Photographs Division, Washington, D.C.
LC-AMED	Courtesy of Library of Congress, African and Middle Eastern Division, Near Eastern Section. Prints and Photographs Division. Washington, D.C.
Mauldin	©1967 by Bill Mauldin. Reprinted courtesy of the Mauldin Estate
MLM	Courtesy of Mme. Martine Laplaine Méric, Louveciennes, France
NYPL	New York Public Library, Microfilm Department , New York City
Ssyn, CSCC	Representing Vicky (Victor Weisz): ©Solo syndication, 17-18 Hayward's Place, London EC 1 ROEQ, England Photo: Centre for the Study of Cartoons and Caricature, Templeman Library, University of Kent, Canterbury, Kent CT2 7NU, England
ST	©Switzerland Tourism New York City

142

INDEX

The interplay of current and historic events required that the Index be both alphabetical and chronological as necessary. Authors quoted are grouped under that heading in the *A* alphabet, rather than by individual names, in order to give a broad view of those who saw the sixties in their special way. A *u* added to an author's entry indicates that the name was not specified on the text page. Book titles and all other quote sources can be found in the Bibliography-Source List, pp. 122-39. Various dates of events, included as a convenience, are a supplement to the Chronology, pp. 9-12. An *italicized* page number indicates an illustrated page, while one in **bold type** refers to a current update or comparison to an event that occurred in the sixties, as discussed in the Epilogue, pp.116-19.

144

149